Beowulf

The Poetry of Legend: Classics of the Medieval World

Beowulf

TRANSLATED AND INTRODUCED
BY
KEVIN CROSSLEY-HOLLAND

CONTENTS

Beowulf

THE POEM

INTRODUCTION

The voices of the past sing all around us. They sing within us. And such is our hunger for historical knowledge and, in particular, knowledge of cultural roots, that we find them endlessly beguiling.

This hunger cannot entirely be ascribed to simple curiosity. It is also the result of the terrible damage that the twentieth century has inflicted on itself. World wars, nuclear hazard, unemployment and epidemic: this old world shakes itself until its bones rattle:

> Pity the planet, all joy gone
> from this sweet volcanic cone;
> peace to our children when they fall
> in small war on the heels of small
> war . . .

(Robert Lowell)

Insecure in themselves and confronted by an uncertain future, people are looking over their shoulders in search of inspiration, continuity and belonging.

In Great Britain and America, the six slow centuries between the time when the Romans resigned themselves to the loss of England from the Empire (at the beginning of the fifth century) and the arrival of the Normans (in the middle of the eleventh century) have now come in for the very closest attention. We have learned to recognize the harsh, splendid and compelling Anglo-Saxon culture both as a brilliant achievement in its own right, and as formative of much that followed it. The Anglo-Saxons were very much the most sophisticated people in early medieval Europe (the time sometimes called the Dark Ages), producing stunning literature, jewellery and illuminated manuscripts. And today, they still stand in the shadows behind many aspects of our lives: our monarchy, our legal and coinage systems, the very look of this land of little villages, and, most important of all, the language used throughout the English-speaking world.

Wherever the English have travelled as pilgrims, crusaders, merchants, colonists and administrators, they have taken with them English attitudes and institutions, some of them later adopted and adapted by indigenous populations; and because England herself has been a country of quite remarkably uninterrupted continuities, many of these same attitudes and institutions have their origins in Anglo-Saxon England.

Only thirty thousand lines of verse survive from Anglo-Saxon times – no more, playing games with numbers, than fifty lines for each year of the Anglo-Saxon period, and overall no more than three times the length of *Paradise Lost.* Natural decay and rats and fanatical censors: time has done its worst.

We can count ourselves fortunate, however, that the

surviving poems are immensely varied in subject matter and tone and, so far as we can tell, date of composition. They include secular heroic poetry, poetry which is elegiac in tone revolving around the themes of transience and the loss of a loved one, quasi-philosophical poetry encapsulating lore and wisdom, and a great deal of religious poetry.

Above all, there is *Beowulf*! This is the stirring and wonderfully readable poem that has at its heart a true hero – not just a man who like every other is entitled to his fifteen minutes of fame, and not a man of action with an empty heart and the mind of an imbecile, but a superman who backs up his quite extraordinary feats with a powerful sense of social responsibility and morality.

Beowulf swims for seven days on the open sea and uses a sword to ward off whales; he grapples hand to hand with a terrifying monster and then dives down under a lake and wrestles with the monster's mother; and in old

A fire-breathing dragon on a gold pendant. The Anglo-Saxon fascination with dragons made them popular images on artefacts.

age, he engages with a fire-breathing dragon. While he certainly glories in these achievements, he does all he does in the name of friendship, and out of a sense of care for his people. The action of the poem is furious, but the character of Beowulf himself is engaging and humane. The very last words of the poem (and their position indicates the importance their poet attached to them) describe its hero in these terms:

> *cwaedon thaet he waere   wyruld-cyninga,*
> *manna mildust   ond mon-thwaerust,*
> *leodum lithost   ond lof-geornost.*

> *they said that of all kings on earth*
> *he was the kindest, the most gentle,*
> *the most just to his people, the most eager for fame.*

Beowulf has had so many claims and statements stacked around it that it sometimes seems in danger of disappearing altogether. It is somehow intimidating to be told that it is not only the greatest surviving Anglo-Saxon poem and the greatest poem in the first one thousand years of our literature, but also the only complete epic poem in any pre-Conquest Germanic language. And today, the hive of critical industry buzzes with arguments and analyses even more loudly than it did when J. R. R. Tolkien offered his famous summary of *Beowulf* criticism fifty years ago:

> Beowulf *is a half-baked native epic . . . it is the confused product of a committee of muddle-headed and probably beer-bemused Anglo-Saxons (this is a Gallic voice); it is a string of pagan lays edited by monks; it is the work of a learned but*

inaccurate Christian antiquarian; it is a work of genius, rare and surprising in the period, though the genius seems to have been shown principally in doing something very much better left undone (this is a very recent voice); it is a wild folk-tale (general chorus); it is a poem of an aristocratic and courtly tradition (same voices); it is a hotch-potch; it is a sociological, anthropological, archaeological document . . .

and so on. The risk is plain: it is that in the end one may not see the wood for the trees; it is that a glorious poem will become ossified and unread. The danger is perfectly summed up in the critic William Alfred's remark that *Beowulf* is 'a national monument as well as a poem'.

So the purpose of this book is quite simply to introduce and present *Beowulf* anew. The editorial material is elucidatory (time has put some obstacles in the reader's path), clearing the way for a close reading of the poem. The images, meanwhile, help not only to relate the poem to contemporary art and artefact but have also been chosen as a mood-commentary. But the poem is the point of the book and the poem is at the heart of it. To read it is to be caught up in an absorbing story and to find oneself in the company of a very considerable poet, a warm and sophisticated storyteller who knows his own mind and

speaks with real authority about fundamental human values. For all that it is anchored in a specific far-off time and place, *Beowulf* tells us an unconscionable amount about ourselves.

Readers may also find, with some sense of shock, that *Beowulf* is very much a poem for our own times. Like the Norse mythology (and *Beowulf* and the ice-bright myths belong to the same pre-Conquest north-west European world), the poem portrays a society in which individuals are not entirely in control of their own fate, and in which there are terrible forces abroad, the worst of which cannot be overcome even by the greatest of men – or not, at least, without the sacrifice of his own life. Confronted by agents of appalling destruction, man must find salvation in his own wits and derring-do, and never compromise his dignity.

Here, then, is an heroic and humane poem; a mirror held to Anglo-Saxon society; a tale belonging to everyone who lives in, or ultimately comes from, the north-west corner of Europe; a story with quite startling contemporary relevance: all these epithets are true of *Beowulf*.

THE HISTORICAL BACKGROUND

The theatre of *Beowulf* is Denmark and part of Sweden. The poem begins and ends in Geatland which is, broadly speaking, that part of Sweden to the south of Lake Vättern, while Beowulf's visit to the court of King Hrothgar at Heorot, and his deadly encounters with Grendel and his mother, take him to Denmark's principal island of Zealand.

The frequent digressions in the poem, however, considerably extend the poem's geography. There is action offstage, as it were, involving a number of tribes and small kingdoms situated in central Sweden (the Swedes), the remainder of Denmark (the Jutes) and northern Germany, Poland and the Low Countries.

There is not a scrap of historical evidence that Beowulf himself ever existed. Possible models and analogues are discussed in 'The Literary Background', but it seems likely the character of Beowulf was essentially the product of the poet's own imagination.

The *Beowulf*-poet was, however, deeply interested in history, and in effect fitted the fairy-tale figure of Beowulf not only into an existing place but into a precise historical context. The poem begins by identifying the lineage of the Danish royal house, and contains a number of historical figures.

The king of the Geats, Hygelac, for instance, is mentioned by the late sixth-century historian Gregory of Tours: he says Hygelac (whom he calls Chlochilaichus) won a battle at Ravenswood in about AD 510 and was killed while attacking the Frisians in about AD 521. Similarly, there are decent grounds for believing that Hrothgar, king of the Danes, and Ongentheow and Haethcyn and Onela and Heardred were all historical characters, and that the great hall Heorot, 'of whose splendours men would always speak', once astonished and delighted everyone who set eyes on it.

Two characters in the poem may have had especial interest for the poet's English audience. One is Offa, the

A striking representation of an Anglo-Saxon king, taken from a belt-buckle, carved in silver-gilt with rich decorations of gold and garnets.

11

fourth-century king of the Angles who tames his wife, Thryth. He also appears in the Anglo-Saxon poem 'Widsith' and several critics have speculated that his inclusion in *Beowulf*, which otherwise seems rather superfluous, is the poet's way of paying a compliment to Offa's descendant and namesake, King Offa of Mercia, who reigned from 757 until 796. This line of thought is based on the presupposition that the poem was composed in eighth-century Mercia.

The other character is Hengest, who succeeds Hnaef as leader of the Half-Danes and after a winter of discontent avenges his death by killing Finn, king of the Frisians. It is perfectly possible that this Hengest, who also appears in the Anglo-Saxon lay known as 'The Finnesburh Fragment', was the same Hengest who came to England with another leader, Horsa, in AD 449 at the invitation of King Vortigern to fight against the Picts; the same Hengest who, as *The Anglo-Saxon Chronicle* (the most important single historical source for the period) reports, then rounded on Vortigern and the Britons, won great battles, and instigated the kingdom of Kent. As the first recorded Anglo-Saxon settler in England, this Hengest would have been of considerable interest to any later Anglo-Saxon audience.

By henching round the character of Beowulf with historical characters and battles, and by setting the poem in carefully specified geographical territory, the poet seems to lend greater weight to his hero's achievements. Both this feature of the poem and the way in which the poet goes into such detail in his depiction of heroic society have

the effect of underpinning deeds and derring-do that might otherwise seem merely fanciful. Fights against two monsters and a dragon are the stuff of legend and folk-tale; but the historical allusions and social realism surrounding them are one reason why *Beowulf* is neither legend nor folk-tale but epic.

Inlaid jewels and circular designs are typical of Anglo-Saxon art. This brooch was made in south-east England.

Although *Beowulf* is so firmly placed in early sixth-century Sweden and Denmark, it is a product of Anglo-Saxon England. The political and cultural world portrayed in it is just as Anglo-Saxon as the world of Shakespeare's historical plays is Elizabethan England.

The question of just when and where *Beowulf* was composed is discussed on p. 29, but, irrespective of which alternative we may prefer, the audience which first heard the poem lived in a land of little kingdoms. The country was divided into seven territories, the chief among them Northumbria, Mercia, East Anglia and Wessex. These kingdoms lived uneasily together; indeed, they fought against each other as well as against tribes waiting in the wings – Britons and Picts, Scots and Strathclyde Welsh. The portrayal in *Beowulf*, therefore, of Geatland and Denmark as two great rival kingdoms, and reference to nagging feuds between these kingdoms and many other tribes, is a feature of the north-west European Germanic world with which the Anglo-Saxons would have been entirely at home.

The Ormside bowl from Cumbria carries the same patterning as the brooch opposite, though separated geographically and by over three hundred years.

Beowulf has scarcely begun before we hear how Hrothgar ensured his followers' support by winning famous victories, and as it ends, we see Beowulf's followers riding round his barrow and eulogizing him. In between, both in set pieces and asides, the poet often returns to the matter of how a king or a lord should treat his followers, and what in return the lord may expect of them. To take no more than a couple of examples: Hrothgar rewards Beowulf for ridding him of the two monsters with many generous gifts, including a sword and a banner, a helmet and a corslet, eight horses with gold-plated bridles and his own superb saddle, inlaid with jewels; and when Beowulf returns home, he gives these

treasures to his own king, Hygelac, and in return Hygelac gives him a sword that belonged to Hrethel, Beowulf's own grandfather, and no less than seven thousand hides of land.

Such scenes tell us much about the nature of power, and the obligations of lord and follower, in Anglo-Saxon England. Power was followers and power was the wealth to keep those followers loyal by giving them treasure (meaning weapons and rings) and land. *Beowulf* puts colourful clothing on the axis of Anglo-Saxon society: the relationship between leader and led founded in the idea of mutual service, and celebrated in a number of Anglo-Saxon poems, such as 'The Wanderer' and 'The Battle of Maldon'.

The *Beowulf*-poet always seems to have time to stop and lovingly describe a weapon – a sword that has its own name and pedigree, a helmet surmounted by a boar-crest, a grey-tipped forest of ash-spears. And when Beowulf's

An ornamented section from a sword hilt, each weapon had its own character.

13

little band lie down in gloomy Heorot on the night when Grendel's mother will descend on the hall, the poet tells how the men put their shields and helmets and corslets and spears at their heads and notes that

> *It was their habit,*
> *both at home and in the field,*
> *to be prepared for battle always . . .*

This is the authentic voice of Anglo-Saxon society. Its password is vigilance, its greatest treasures are weapons, and its central preoccupation is war.

Anglo-Saxon England of the seventh and eighth centuries was by no means wholly Christian. Augustine's mission arrived in Kent in AD 597 and the rapid spread of Celtic Christianity in Northumbria took place during the second part of the seventh century. But many

A detail from a Danish gilt brooch. The face resembles an Old Testament prophet and demonstrates how easily Christian imagery was assimilated to existing forms.

communities committed apostasy when frightened by a plague, or a famine, or an eclipse, while Raedwald, King of East Anglia, wanted to set up an altar to Christ alongside those to the old gods; and many communities, one suspects, scarcely took aboard Christianity at all.

The sheer inconsistency of the Christian element in *Beowulf* seems consistent with what we know of Anglo-Saxon England at the time of its composition. It is true that Grendel and his mother are said to be descendants of Cain, and that Beowulf is Christian, but the Danes are portrayed both as heathen and Christian, and Beowulf is shown also to be in the hands of inexorable fate. 'Fate', says the poet in a famous half-line, 'goes ever as it must'. How would the poet have reconciled such apparent opposites? Would he perhaps have agreed with a later Anglo-Saxon poet who argued that 'fate moves in the mind of God'? And was he even particularly interested in such matters?

No matter how one answers these and similar questions, which are discussed in 'How to Read the Poem', it should be remembered that early sixth-century Scandinavia was heathen from top to toe. The *Beowulf*-poet, however, has portrayed a society in which worship of the old gods and the new god – a new god, let it be said, with a decidedly Old Testament flavour – live in tandem. In this, as in his depiction of feuding kingdoms and the central relationship of lord and follower, he has in fact truthfully portrayed his own society.

TIME CHART

Though the *Beowulf* poem is timeless, drawing material from the wealth of Anglo-Saxon culture and from many countries, the timechart sets it in a historical perspective. The period between the departure of the Roman army from Britain and the Battle of Hastings was a turbulent one, full of wars, uncertainty and changing ideas. To help the reader gain a fuller understanding of the poem the major events of the age are listed below. *Beowulf* is partly a chronicle of these exciting times.

Names in italics are alluded to in Beowulf

AD

98	Tacitus writes *Germania*.
410	The fall of Roman Britain.
449	*Hengest* and Horsa come to England at the invitation of Vortigern, king of the Britons.
455	Hengest and Horsa kill Vortigern.
c.510	The *Battle of Ravenswood*.
c.518	*Ingeld* marries *Freawaru*.
c.520	*Heorot* burnt to the ground.
c.521	*Hygelac* killed in battle against the *Frisians*.
c.533	*Onela* invades Geatland and kills *Heardred*.
563	St. Columba's foundation of Iona.
594	Death of Gregory of Tours.
597	Augustine sent by Pope Gregory to Britain.
624 or	
625	Death of Raedwald, king of the East Anglia. Probable date of Sutton Hoo ship-burial.
627	Bishop Paulinus visits Edwin, king of Northumbria.
664	Synod of Whitby.
673–735	Life of the Venerable Bede.
680	Caedmon's vision.
757–96	Reign of Offa, king of Mercia.
766–814	Reign of Charlemagne, king of the Franks.
787	First Viking raids on England.
793	Vikings attack Lindisfarne.
871–99	Reign of Alfred, king of Wessex.
c.892	Compilation of *The Anglo-Saxon Chronicle* (drawing on earlier documents).
991	The Battle of Maldon.
c.1000	Compilation of manuscript which includes *Beowulf*.
1066	The Battle of Hastings.

THE SOCIAL BACKGROUND

The poet who composed *Beowulf* had wide-ranging interests, a subtle mind, and a very well-developed sense of right and wrong. He thought it entirely proper not only to entertain but also to instruct. At one level, the poem is a kind of supernatural thriller; but at another, it is a moral commentary which tells us an enormous amount about Anglo-Saxon day-to-day life, attitudes and beliefs.

This willingness to pronounce, and to teach, is not peculiar to the *Beowulf*-poet. It is one of the primary strands in the fabric of Anglo-Saxon poetry, and indeed characteristic of any society for whom poetry is not an enigma or a luxury but an authority, a point of reference, and a vital force.

The poet's method is sometimes direct, sometimes indirect. Most telling, maybe, and certainly most pithy, are his half-line comments with which he rounds off a description of some scene or action. 'That was a loyal band of retainers,' he says, and 'They knew the customs of warriors', and 'Make good use of everything'. Sometimes the poet praises or reproves at greater length, and sometimes he allows one of his characters to speak for him. When Hrothgar tells Beowulf that Grendel's mother has exacted vengeance for the death of her son, Beowulf replies

Do not grieve, wise Hrothgar! Better each man
should avenge his friend than deeply mourn.
The days on earth for every one of us
are numbered; he who may should win renown
before his death; that is a warrior's
best memorial when he has departed from this world . . .
Shoulder your sorrows with patience
this day; this is what I expect of you.

Who, hearing these noble and authoritative lines, does not believe that they express the poet's own views? We meet, in the *Beowulf*-poet, a man equally interested in the worlds of action and of ideas, apparently untroubled by self-doubt. He has much to say about both personal and public

This matrix, used to make helmet plates, shows a ritual scene being acted out by two figures. Features from nature combine with human passions in a world where the two were closely linked.

17

life, and his images and words endure and glitter like granite.

In 'The Historical Background', I noted several of the scenes in which the poet presents and comments on the relationship between lord and follower. This relationship is the poem's most powerful *leitmotif*, and it is explored in many different aspects. The poet tells us that to secure followers a young man must have mettle and be generous. We hear how the ten lily-livered oath-breakers who desert Beowulf when he is assailed by the dragon are chastised

The threads of Anglo-Saxon kinship seem to be reflected in the swirling shapes of this manuscript illustration.

for their disloyalty. We see how Hnaef is unable to follow Finn, the slayer of his lord; all winter he broods on vengeance, and in the spring he strikes. In these and very many other scenes the relationship of lord and follower is shown as central to the Anglo-Saxon experience.

But scarcely less important to the *Beowulf*-poet, as to the society from which he sprang, are the claims of kinship. To enter the world of *Beowulf* is somewhat akin to visiting a quite small and self-referring community – like, say, the island of Iceland – where almost everybody seems to be related to one another. There is often more to a situation than first meets the eye because all kinds of obligations motivate the behaviour of the protagonists. As soon as he reaches Heorot, Beowulf tells Hrothgar that he has come because he is the one man who can dispose of the monster Grendel, and this is partly true; but Hrothgar sees Beowulf's timely arrival as being the proper repayment by a son of favours earlier bestowed on his father. Again, when Wiglaf comes to the support of Beowulf, fighting the dragon and in terrible danger, he is mindful of his obligations not only as a follower but as a blood-cousin of the old king. 'The claims of kinship', observes the poet, 'can never be ignored by a right-minded man.'

Writing at the end of the first century about Germanic tribesmen within the Roman Empire, the precursors of the first settlers in England, the Roman historian Tacitus makes two important observations. 'As for leaving a battle alive, after your chief has fallen,' he writes 'that means lifelong infamy and shame. To defend and protect him, to put down one's own acts of heroism to

A furious battle scene from a Swedish standing stone. No matter what the outcome, a warrior was under a binding obligation to stand by his chief.

his credit – that is what they really mean by allegiance. The chiefs fight for victory, the companions for their chief.' And secondly, 'A man is bound to take up the feuds as well as the friendships of father and kinsmen'.

Add to these cornerstone comments the passionate scenes of loyalty (and treachery) in such secular heroic poems as 'The Finnesburh Fragment' and 'The Battle of Maldon' (which describes a fierce encounter between Anglo-Saxons and Vikings in 991), and the dry but crackling reports from *The Anglo-Saxon Chronicle*, and it is clear that *Beowulf* is well in line with other literary sources in its emphasis on kinship and the relationship of lord and follower. But it is only in *Beowulf*, by far the longest of the surviving secular heroic poems, that these relationships are explored in the round.

A preoccupation with conflict, whether family feud or pitched battle, naturally implies both resolve and physical bravery. Indeed, these are qualities implicit in Tacitus' observations and regularly admired by Anglo-Saxon poets. In 'The Battle of Maldon', the old warrior Byrhtwold, surrounded by Viking warriors, calls out:

> *Mind must be the firmer, heart the more fierce,*
> *courage the greater, as our strength diminishes.*
> *Here lies our leader, hewn down,*
> *an heroic man in the dust.*
> *He who now longs to escape will lament for ever.*
> *I am old. I will not go from here,*
> *but I mean to lie by the side of my lord,*
> *lie in the dust with the man I loved so dearly.*

The poet who composed *Beowulf* would have admired sentiments such as these. The strong should be praised, he says, and that praise may outlive them; the weak, meanwhile, go to the wall. The strong maintain the fabric of society; the weak, like the 'ten cowardly oath-breakers' who abandon Beowulf, undermine it and are deserving only of contempt and exile. To be strong in mind and strong in body: 'Such', says the poet, 'should a man, a thane, be in time of necessity!'

The Anglo-Saxon settlers who came to England in the fifth century did not know how to build with brick or stone. Their building materials were wood and wattle-and-daub with reeds for roofing. They called the Romans 'giants' precisely because they did know how to use stone, and the eighth-century poem 'The Ruin' is an eulogy of the extensive Roman city at Bath. There is one fleeting reference to stonework in *Beowulf*, and here too the tone is one of wonder: the dying Beowulf turns to the rock cavern which was the dragon's lair and 'gazed at the work of giants, / saw how the ancient earthwork contained/ stone arches supported by columns'.

The early Anglo-Saxons, however, were capable of erecting very substantial half-timbered buildings, as several recent excavations have confirmed. The seventh-century royal hall excavated at Yeavering in the Cheviots, for instance, was built to what is known as a 'three-aisled double square plan' and measured eighty feet by forty feet. The oak walls were almost six inches thick, and as the timbers were set eight feet into the ground, it seems the hall was as high as it was long, wide and handsome.

The *Beowulf*-poet has plenty to tell us about the building of the great hall Heorot. It is not glorious by accident: from the first, King Hrothgar intended that it should be the greatest of all halls, lofty and wide-gabled,

A hall was the focus of community life; King Hrothgar was reduced to despair when the splendid Heorot was lost to Grendel. Beowulf was first sung and recited between such timbered walls.

'braced inside and out with hammered iron bands'. And not only is the hall structurally prepossessing; it is also lavishly furnished and decorated. The poet says admiringly that it contains mead benches inlaid with gold, and that there are horns and tapestries hanging on the walls. Here, as elsewhere, his regard for the functionally beautiful is plain to see.

Heorot is the heart of King Hrothgar's kingdom, and the poet gives us an incomparable picture of all the activities conducted within it. This picture may be idealized, but the poet was speaking out of his own experience. The administrative and social activities that take place in Heorot are representative of what was going on in the halls of kings and ealdormen the length and breadth of England.

At the administrative level, the hall was used as a kind of glorified office. Discussion of problems and possible courses of action did not take place in ante-rooms; they were rehearsed on the floor. The hall was in daily use as the centre for matters of personnel, the maintenance of law and order in the district, estate management, supervision of the household, and the reception of visitors. When Beowulf and his band of Geats arrive at the court of Hrothgar, they are advised to leave their shields and ashen spears outside Heorot, and are then led into the hall itself to meet Hrothgar, surrounded by his thanes, and to explain why they have come to Denmark.

But, as *Beowulf* so colourfully shows us, the hall was also the court's social hub. In Heorot the lord distributes rings (just as symbolic then as they are today) and treasure

Drinking horns were lavishly decorated with many different materials. This detail in burnished gold shows a horned god surrounded with star designs. Along with weapons, horns were highly prized possessions.

the auroch, the extinct wild ox of northern Europe, had a capacity of six quarts; but as we see in *Beowulf*, the feasters also used drinking-cups, made of metal or pottery and inlaid with precious stones.

After the feast, the principal entertainer was the storytelling poet. With a fine sense of drama, the *Beowulf*-poet ranges his audience alongside the 'brutish demon' Grendel in the outer darkness, day after day listening to

> *the din of merry-making*
> *inside the hall, and the sound of the harp*
> *and the bard's clear song . . .*

It is not so difficult to imagine *Beowulf* itself being recited or sung in this way. The poet gets up from the mead-bench and goes to the poet's place opposite his lord and by the fire. He adds a log to the fire. He takes his little lyre-like harp, his six-stringer made of maple with poplar or willow pegs, out of its beaver-skin bag:

> *one of Hrothgar's thanes*
> *who brimmed with poetry, and remembered lays,*
> *a man acquainted with ancient traditions*
> *of every kind, composed a new song*
> *in correct metre. Most skilfully that man*
> *began to sing of Beowulf's feat,*
> *to weave words together, and fluently*
> *to tell a fitting tale . . .*

At the centre of the activities in Heorot stands Wealhtheow, influential queen, protective mother and doubtless supervisor of many domestic activities – no light matter in a virtually self-sufficient community – such as

to his followers, thereby ensuring their loyalty to him. And in the hall the lord and his followers and visitors feast and drink. The poet does not say as much but we know they would have been eating bread from the oven, boiled and baked meats, and as principal vegetables rye and beans and peas. In fact, given the Anglo-Saxons' restricted cooking facilities, largely confined to the big pot hanging over the fire in the centre of the hall, it is difficult to resist the conclusion that the Anglo-Saxons largely existed for six centuries on various kinds of stew. For drink, as we learn from the riddles and several other literary sources, there was mead made from fermented honey, ale made from barley, and doubtless all kinds of home-made wine. For the very young, and for those with hangovers (there is no evidence of such a thing as an Anglo-Saxon teetotaller!) there was milk and sweet water from the well. The favoured container was a drinking-horn, and the horn of salting, brewing, spinning, weaving, dyeing and clothes-making.

In his *Germania*, Tacitus writes of the Germanic tribesmen that 'they believe that there resides in women an element of holiness and prophecy, and so they do not scorn to ask their advice or lightly disregard their replies'. Anglo-Saxon literature, meanwhile, shows the society's women variously as heroic companions, pawns given in marriage as 'peace-weavers' between two feuding families, passionate lovers, sex objects, devoted mothers, devout Christians, owners of great estates, slaves . . .

Several of these elements are present in the make-up of Wealhtheow and other women on stage and off-stage (in the digressions) in *Beowulf*. For example, when Beowulf has disposed of Grendel, there is a certain headiness at the Danish court. Twelve years of torment have come to an end. Old Hrothgar not only promises rewards to the Geat but tells him

> *I will love you in my heart*
> *like a son; keep to our new kinship*
> *from this day on.*

It is noteworthy that it is Wealhtheow who steadies the boat at this emotional moment. Speaking as wife, mother and counsellor, and speaking with great dignity, she tells her husband it is right to give rewards but warns him against adopting the Geat and reminds Hrothgar of his responsibilities: 'leave this land and the Danish people/ to your own descendants when the day comes/ for you to die'. Matters of behaviour and procedure are dear to the poet's heart and important to *Beowulf*, and Wealhtheow plays a significant part in determining and executing them.

Nowhere in *Beowulf* is the sense of ritual and decorum more pronounced than in the poem's final scene. The Geats prepare a pyre for the old king up on Whaleness, 'hung round with helmets and shields and shining mail'; a maiden 'with her tresses swept up' keens and then prophesies; the warriors place rings and brooches amongst their lord's ashes, and build a huge barrow over them; then twelve men ride round the barrow . . .

As detail is added to detail, and the poem gravely moves to its close, we feel the separate force of each observance and know these funeral rites to be hallowed by time. For all that Beowulf is professedly Christian, we see him laid to rest in the manner of a great Germanic heroic warrior. We are witnesses at a superb pagan funeral.

Until fifty years ago, critics thought it improbable that even the most lavish of Anglo-Saxon cremations could have borne comparison with Beowulf's funeral. The

A maiden 'with her tresses swept up'. This classical portrait of a woman comes from a fluted silver dish found at the Sutton Hoo ship burial.

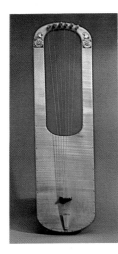

A harp reconstructed from pieces found at Sutton Hoo. This instrument would have accompanied the Bard as he provided the entertainment at a feast. Like most civilised peoples, the Anglo-Saxons had a keen ear for music.

discovery in 1939 of the stunning ship-burial at Sutton Hoo changed all that. Rupert Bruce-Mitford and his team of excavators opened a barrow now believed to have been that of the seventh-century King Raedwald and, working against the clock in the months immediately preceding the outbreak of the Second World War, they lifted from sandy East Suffolk, 'the richest and most brilliant treasure ever found on British soil' (Sir David Wilson).

An enormous gold buckle, silver dishes, a purse-lid jewelled with garnet and enamel, gold shoulder-clasps inlaid with garnets, a shield, a shattered (and now excitingly reconstructed) helmet: these and many other treasures immediately established the sophistication, wealth and Swedish ancestry of the East Anglian royal household. Before long it became clear that almost every artefact—horn and hanging-bowl, sword and harp,

whetstone and winged dragon—had its counterpart in *Beowulf*, and that the treasure thus constituted a kind of commentary on the poem.

Over the years, evaluation of the Sutton Hoo treasure has thrown light on many important aspects of *Beowulf*, including Anglo-Saxon kingship, weaponry and poetry recitation. But even to look at the treasure for the first time, with an innocent eye, is to enter Heorot and the wider world of the *Beowulf*-poet, and to see them all the more vividly.

Conversely, *Beowulf* has thrown light on Sutton Hoo. The first instance of this was also the most dramatic. When the ownership of the hoard was in dispute, the rival claimants being the Crown and Mrs. Pretty, the owner of the land on which the ship-burial was found, two passages from *Beowulf* were read in court. These described the ship-burial of Scyld and the funeral of Beowulf. It was then argued that the Sutton Hoo hoard was not Treasure Trove but belonged to Mrs. Pretty because it was buried in similar circumstances: in public, that is to say, and with no intent to recover it:

> *They buried rings and brooches in the barrow . . .*
> *They bequeathed the gleaming gold, treasure of men,*
> *to the earth, and there it still remains,*
> *as useless to men as it was before.*

Thus art imitates life and life turns to art. Mrs. Pretty won the day and subsequently presented the Sutton Hoo treasure to the British Museum! It is there today, just a few steps away from the *Beowulf* manuscript.

23

At no time in the Anglo-Saxon period was more than a very small percentage of the population literate; a book was a rare and valuable object, painstakingly prepared by monks in monastery scriptoria or by scribes at court.

The Anglo-Saxon poet was, therefore, not only an entertainer but also a memory bank. He (there is no evidence of professional woman-poets in England at this time, though a number of the elegiac poems are dramatic monologues spoken by women) knew the old stories the first settlers had brought with them in the early fifth century from their continental homelands, the legends about Germanic heroes and heroines whose lives constituted historical stepping-stones for their successors and whose behaviour served as examples and warnings.

That part of the canon of Anglo-Saxon poetry known as heroic – or sometimes secular heroic, to distinguish it from poems in which certain Christian saints are given heroic treatment! – contains fragments of these tales and many glancing references to legendary characters such as Weland, the master-smith and Ermanaric (called Eormenric by the *Beowulf*-poet), the tyrant-king of the Goths, who were celebrated in story-song throughout north-west Europe.

Beowulf itself is full of allusions to events and individuals evidently familiar to the poet and his audience. Doubtless each of them was once the subject of many a separate poem now long lost; the extended digression concerning Hengest is quite exceptional in having a counterpart – the brilliant and excited lay known as 'The Finnesburh Fragment'. To read them side by side is not only to see a dramatic episode from two angles but to be reminded that the surviving body of secular heroic poetry must represent no more than a minuscule proportion of the whole canon.

The poet who composed *Beowulf* was working within an oral tradition. Although it is perfectly possible that there was a manuscript of *Beowulf* earlier than that in which it now survives, perhaps even a manuscript made at the time of its composition, the poem is the product of a society that expected to hear poetry, not to read it.

Like the whole body of Anglo-Saxon poetry, *Beowulf* is built of four-stress lines, in which there are a number of possible syllabic patterns, and in which the third stress invariably alliterates with one or both of the first two. The poem draws substantially on a common stock of words and phrases and half-lines. When the poet says, 'I have heard that . . .' he is using a conventional formula, not speaking literally. Likewise, he had at his disposal a large number of synonyms for the most common nouns, essential if he was to maintain the alliterative flow, and a host of compounds and kennings (or condensed metaphors). In one short passage of no more than nineteen lines (page 52), the *Beowulf*-poet uses three synonyms for 'wave', six for 'men' and four for 'boat' (two of which, 'curved-prow' and 'sea-wood', are kennings). The beauty of the passage, which describes a sea-crossing, lies not in the poet's inventive powers but in his mastery of repetition and variation.

These factors – metrical and lexical – mean that Anglo-Saxon poetry is conservative. By conforming to a formula or pattern it preserves it. They also mean that it may not have been necessary for a poet to have undergone extensive training. He was working within quite a rigid grid, producing a poem that was at one and the same time new and derivative. While it is true that some Anglo-Saxon poems rely very heavily on the existing wordhoard and others sing in their chains like the sea, it is unlikely that either the present-day admiration of originality for its own sake or disapproval of plagiarism would have had much meaning for the Anglo-Saxons.

There are surprisingly few references in Anglo-Saxon literature to poetic technique and recitation. The passage from *Beowulf* cited in 'The Social Background' is the fullest surviving description of the process of composition, and it is significant that it lays much emphasis on shaping, and none on originality. The phrase 'singan and secgan' – to sing and say – which occurs in several contexts, may give us a hint as to the manner in which poetry was recited: neither spoken nor sung but intoned or chanted to the accompaniment of the lyre described in the previous section.

References in Anglo-Saxon poetry to a poet's feelings at being displaced in his lord's affections by another man, and to how the poet

> *will settle beside his harp*
> *at his lord's feet, be handed treasures,*
> *and always quickly pluck the strings*
> *with a plectrum . . . Harpist, heart's desire!*

are perhaps indicative of the great skills expected of the professional poet, and the value set on them, but 'amateur' poetry-making was probably just as commonplace as music-making today. In his famous description of how the cowherd Caedmon saw a vision and went on to become the greatest poet of his day, the Venerable Bede says everyone present at a feast 'took it in turns to sing and entertain the company'. Such poems as the riddles, with

A scene from an ivory casket depicting a slave preparing two geese for a feast. Poetry was a natural accompaniment to eating and drinking.

their sharp and often amusing cameos of natural phenomena, animal and bird life and man-made artefacts, would surely have gone down well at an occasion such as this.

The hero Beowulf, in the wonderful words of Gwyn Jones, is 'a wave-piercer, scourge of sea-beasts, cleanser of a house, grappler with a monstrous arm, finder of a wondrous sword, destroyer of giants and mere-wife, to say nothing of dragon-slayer later'. Yet in allusion and digression, this same superman is surrounded by dozens of characters who inhabit the misty world between history and legend: men and women like Ermanaric and Hildeburh, who did once live and breathe but now stand at an angle to history, grown huge in time's afterglow. At times the poet appears to be telling a wondertale, at times he anchors events by reference to specific character, object and event. It is not surprising, therefore, to find that the poem has many sources and analogues.

The first two-thirds of *Beowulf* describe the hero's defeat of the monster Grendel and his terrifying mother. This part of the poem has much in common with a folk-tale, known in slightly differing form in many countries, called 'The Three Stolen Princesses'. In both, there is a hero of supernatural strength (the son of a bear and a woman in the folk-tale); in both the hero comes with companions to a house possessed by a monster; in both a companion suffers before the hero defeats the monster; and in both there is a journey 'through a hole' to an underworld, the discovery of a sword, a second monster

fight . . . We can, therefore, reasonably surmise that *Beowulf* and the folk-tale as it is known in its variants today, derive from the same wonder-tale source (as do several Icelandic analogues) and not from history or legend.

The last part of *Beowulf* describes the old king's fight to the death with the dragon. It is impossible to say where this episode originated, but several Norse accounts of dragon-fights ultimately derive from the same source. In choosing a dragon to be Beowulf's last and greatest adversary, the poet was in step with the northern European tradition that the 'worm', the great serpent so often represented in jewellery and stone-carving, is the most savage of all opponents and so in a sense the most worthy test of a man's moral and physical courage.

Germanic literature is, indeed, strewn with dragons in myth, legend, heroic poem, saga and folk-tale. The Midgard serpent, offspring of Loki, lies in the cold seas that surround our middle-earth, grown so huge that it

Representations of dragons took many forms; these two come from a purse-lid.

encompasses the whole world and bites on his own tail. Fafnir, the magician's son, turns himself into a dragon so as to guard his cursed gold hoard and, as the *Beowulf*-poet tells us, he is killed by Sigemund (Sigurd in Old Norse sources, and in German sources Siegfried). In the British Isles, meanwhile, more than seventy villages have dragon-tales associated with them, ranging from the marvellously named Muckle Mester Stoor Worm and the terrifying Knucker to the dragon who gets his comeuppance in the hilarious ballad of 'The Dragon of Wantley'.

Without exception, the digressions in *Beowulf* (each discussed separately in the *Notes*) have their roots in Germanic history and legend; it is often impossible to draw a line between the two. The analogues are legion. *Beowulf* begins, for instance, by describing the arrival over the sea, heroic life and ship-burial of the legendary Scyld Scefing, founder of the Danish nation – and there are references to Scyld in *The Anglo-Saxon Chronicle* (where Scyld is shown as an ancestor of a king of Wessex), and in a contemporary biography of King Alfred, and in Danish histories and Icelandic sagas, while a *Chronicle Roll* dating from the reign of King Henry VI of England (1429–71) tells us that Scyld 'was the first man to inhabit Germany'.

A number of the principal protagonists in *Beowulf* – though not, as discussed elsewhere, Beowulf himself – are mentioned in other Dark Age sources. Almost every stage of the story has its parallel elsewhere in early medieval Germanic literature. The matter of sources and analogues may be a complex one, but to be aware of them is to see

this early English poem, rooted partly in folk-tale and partly in history and legend, as belonging to a mighty northern European tradition.

*B*eowulf survives in only one manuscript (*c.* AD 1000) and there is no reference to it or its hero in any other source. Its bedfellows are three prose pieces about fantastic monsters and marvels, and the splendid poem 'Judith' in which the heroine lops off Holofernes' head and carts it away in a bag. So it appears that the late Anglo-Saxons did not see *Beowulf* so much as a great masterpiece as a weird and wonderful monster story.

The manuscript in question is Cotton Vitellius A.XV in the British Museum. It derives part of its name from the Elizabethan antiquary Sir Robert Cotton, and once formed part of his prodigious library. The whereabouts of the manuscript between the eleventh and sixteenth centuries is not known, but it was probably on the shelves of one of the many great monastic libraries dispersed after Henry VIII's Dissolution of the Monasteries. Cotton Vitellius A.XV is not particularly prepossessing: it measures about eight inches by five and was the work of two scribes writing in West Saxon dialect; some of its pages were scorched in the fire which damaged the library in 1731 and on some pages letters and whole words have crumbled away or faded.

The author of *Beowulf*, as of the great majority of Anglo-Saxon poems, is unknown. It could have been composed by a poet working at court, and it could have been composed by a poet-monk: which alternative you prefer largely depends on how you view the function of Christianity within the poem.

The difficult questions of date and place of composition are best considered in tandem. It is clear *Beowulf* could not have been composed before AD 521 because of reference in the poem to the death of Hygelac, nor later than *c*. AD 1000 because that is the date of the manuscript. But where are we to assign it within this period of almost five hundred years? Some critics have argued for the seventh century on the grounds that the *Beowulf*-poet alludes to, and expects his audience to be fully conversant with, many Germanic characters and legends that would have been forgotten in later times; some have preferred the seventh or eighth centuries because the Anglo-Saxons might not have wanted to hear a poem about Danes and Geats at the time (beginning in AD 787) when they were on the receiving end of Viking raids; and, recently, some critics have created a stir by suggesting a date as late as the tenth century.

The majority view is that *Beowulf* dates from the eighth century, but to be more precise depends on where one believes the poem to have been composed.

There are three contenders. Northumbria during the dynamic and sophisticated Age of Bede (AD 680–730) was once a clear frontrunner, but is now perhaps the least highly favoured. Mercia during the brilliant reign of King Offa (AD 757–796) is certainly a possibility, and necessarily the winner if one believes the Offa-digression in *Beowulf* (see p. 102) to be the poet's way of praising his patron. The third contender, East Anglia, has come seriously into the reckoning as a result of the Sutton Hoo discovery, which dates from approximately AD 625. Not only was the ship-burial uncannily like the burials of Scyld and Beowulf: the grave-goods revealed the East Anglian court of the Wuffing dynasty to be unexpectedly sophisticated, and also established definite links between the Wuffings and the Swedish royal house at Uppsala.

It is now thought possible that these two dynasties had a common ancestry. 'Was it through the early East Anglian court', asks the *Beowulf*-scholar Howell Chickering, 'that detailed knowledge of Scandinavian tribal history in *Beowulf* became available in England?' And was the poem, one might add, composed as a way of telling East Anglians something about their half-historical, half-legendary Scandinavian forebears? There is a good case for believing that *Beowulf* was composed in Suffolk, at the palace of Rendlesham, within living memory of the great ship-burial in AD 625.

HOW TO READ THE POEM

Life, as perceived by the inhabitants of pre-Christian northern Europe, was a dazzle of light between darkness and darkness. Both Anglo-Saxons and Vikings, it is true, allowed and even provided for the possibility of a finite afterlife, but both threw emphasis on the brevity of human life and both emphasized how important it was for a person to live in such a way that, if nothing else, his name and good works would live after him. 'One thing I know never dies nor changes,' goes an Old Norse proverb: 'the reputation of a dead man'; while the Anglo-Saxon poet who composed the elegiac poem 'The Seafarer' spoke of the inevitability of death by 'illness or old age or the sword's edge' and exhorted each and every man to 'strive, before he leaves this world, to win the praise of those living after him'.

These are the ideas underlying the solemn and noble scene at the very end of *Beowulf*. Twelve warriors ride round their dead leader's barrow; they talk between themselves about the old king, reviewing his life and works, and the poet tells us that

> *it is fitting for a man,*
> *when his lord and friend must leave this life,*
> *to mouth words in his praise*
> *and to cherish his memory.*

We know very little, alas, of Anglo-Saxon mythology, but across the North Sea the Vikings viewed not only life but the existence of the world itself as caught between darkness and darkness, or, perhaps more accurately, nothingness and nothingness. The Norse mythology portrays a world created in the huge void of Ginnungagap, where ice from the north meets fire from the south; and, uniquely fatalistic, it prophesies a time when all creation will rise up in mutually destructive conflict. Gods and men will fight against giants and monsters and all creation will be wiped out.

The relationship of Christianity to this uncompromising and bleak viewpoint was perfectly described by the Venerable Bede, the Northumbrian historian whose lifespan may have overlapped that of the *Beowulf*-poet. In his *History of the English Church and People*, he recounts how Bishop Paulinus put the case for Christianity to King Edwin of Northumbria and his council, and how in the subsequent discussion one counsellor said:

> *Your Majesty, when we compare the present life of man with that time of which we have no knowledge, it seems to me like the swift flight of a lone sparrow through the banqueting-hall where you sit in the winter months to dine with your thanes and counsellors. Inside there is a comforting fire to warm the*

31

Detail from an Anglo-Saxon cross in Derbyshire. The saint shown here could easily be a pagan god or character from folk-lore. Ideas flowed freely between Christianity and the existing religions, as the former accommodated the latter.

room; outside, the wintry storms of snow and rain are raging. This sparrow flies swiftly in through one door of the hall, and out through another. While he is inside, he is safe from winter storms; but after a few moments of comfort, he vanishes from sight into the darkness whence he came. Similarly, man appears on earth for a little while, but we know nothing of what went before this life, and what follows. Therefore if this new teaching can reveal any more certain knowledge, it seems only right that we should follow it.

Here, too, we are shown in the most graphic terms a world caught between darkness and darkness, but now that darkness is penetrated by a new message and a new hope.

Irrespective of how convinced a Christian the *Beowulf*-poet was (or was not), we would do well to set the structure of the poem alongside these Norse and Anglo-Saxon perceptions of existence. When the poem opens, the Danish court of King Hrothgar is seen to be in the darkness of despair: for twelve years it has been in the grip of an appalling monster. With the arrival of Beowulf, everything changes. The hero wrenches off Grendel's arm and then kills Grendel's mother. Happiness and harmony are restored to Heorot.

When Beowulf returns home to Geatland, and succeeds to the throne, the enemies of the Geats – notably the Swedes – are pushed into the wings. No one can withstand the hero and for a while there is peace in Geatland, as now in Denmark. But no sooner has the old king been mortally wounded in his last great fight with the dragon than the poet brings the forces of darkness back onto the stage. The messenger who announces Beowulf's death to the Geats, says

> *Henceforth, fingers must grasp,*
> *hands must hold, many a spear*
> *chill with the cold of morning; no sound of the harp*
> *shall rouse the warriors but, craving for carrion,*
> *the dark raven shall have its say*
> *and tell the eagle how it fared at the feast*
> *when, competing with the wolf, it laid bare the bones*
> *of corpses*

In the same spirit, a Geatish maiden at Beowulf's funeral repeatedly intones a dirge and then

> *declared she lived in dread of days to come*
> *dark with carnage and keening, terror of the enemy,*
> *humiliation and captivity.*

Beowulf's achievement has been to create an oasis of light. He has kept murder and mayhem at bay. And now that he is dead, darkness will close in once more. It may help us to a better understanding of the poet's intentions and the poem's meaning to recognize that the structure of *Beowulf* is cyclical in the same manner as the Norse myth alluded to above. The coming darkness is redeemed by no new message or new hope. Beowulf's companions do not pray for his soul; they grieve at his death and perpetuate his memory:

> *they said that of all kings on earth*
> *he was the kindest, the most gentle,*
> *the most just to his people, the most eager for fame.*

The question of how to interpret the Christian element in *Beowulf* is one much fought over by critics, and the way you resolve it will certainly have bearing on your 'reading' or understanding of the poem.

An Anglo-Saxon pendant in the form of a Christian cross uses inlaid garnets and fine carving to produce an object of intrinsic beauty.

When the poet castigates the Danes for their worship of 'idols in their pagan tabernacles' and asserts that 'Joy shall be his/ who, when he dies, may stand before the Lord,/ seek peace in the embrace of the Father', we can, I think, be certain that he is himself a Christian. But that is just about as far as agreement goes, and difficulties are compounded by the many ambiguities and apparent inconsistencies within the poem.

The same Danes censured for their pagan practices are also shown as listening to the poet singing

> *that the Almighty made the earth,*
> *this radiant plain encompassed by oceans:*
> *and that God, all powerful, ordained*
> *sun and moon to shine for mankind,*
> *adorned all regions of the world*
> *with trees and leaves.*

Similarly, Beowulf himself is portrayed in two suits of clothing. When he tells Hrothgar about his hazardous underwater meeting with Grendel's mother, he says 'our encounter would have ended at once if God/ had not guarded me', and yet the same man is also the subject of a full-blown pagan funeral. Many attempts have been made to find a framework for the poem that accounts for and accommodates this kind of difficulty.

There are very few specifically Christian references within *Beowulf* and not a single mention of Christ or one of the great Christian dogmas. Rather, the poet turns for reference to the Old Testament: Grendel, for instance, is identified as 'one of the seed of Cain'. But this has not stopped some critics from seeing Beowulf as a kind of

Christ-figure. The poem's greatest editor, Fr. Klaeber, wrote that, 'We might even feel inclined to recognize features of the Christian Saviour in the destroyer of hellish fiends, the warrior brave and gentle, blameless in thought and deed, the king that dies for his people'; while M. B. McNamee has taken things one step further and argued that the poem is an allegory describing the Salvation of Man, Christ's Resurrection and the Harrowing of Hell and Christ's death.

The early Christian missionaries in England put a lot of emphasis on the books of the Old Testament, because the pagan Anglo-Saxons responded easily to its tribal and warlike aspect. Much Anglo-Saxon Christian poetry has a heroic emphasis: Satan is shown as a faithless retainer, and

A contemporary carving of a Christian missionary holding his crosier. Preaching to the unconverted was often perilous and demanded great courage.

in *The Dream of the Rood* Christ himself voluntarily strips and climbs up on to the Cross. The Old Testament references in *Beowulf* have suggested to some critics that

we should see the poem as the work of a Christian poet interested in discovering affinities between Christian and pre-Christian values. Thus Kenneth Sisam wrote: 'In *Beowulf* there is little that is distinctively Christian in the strict sense. The words and conduct of the ideal characters are for the most part designed to show qualities such as courage, loyalty, generosity, and wisdom, which are admired by good men of any creed. Other characteristics, such as determination to exact vengeance, are not in accord with Christian doctrine, but were probably still admired by the majority of Anglo-Saxons in Christian times.'

It is not far from here to J. R. R. Tolkien's view that the poet was a Christian antiquarian who did not have an expressly Christian purpose in composing *Beowulf*, but was attempting 'to depict ancient pre-Christian days, intending to emphasize their nobility, and the desire of the good for truth'. But some critics, following Tolkien's lead, have not been so certain that the poet wholeheartedly

Two dragons decorate a ring belonging to the Anglo-Saxon king, Athelwulf.

admired the world he portrays, and detected weaknesses in both Beowulf himself and the code by which he lives. Thus Beowulf has been found guilty of arrogance and gold-greed in his last fight with the dragon. The wise reader will look at the whole poem, and the poet's characterization of Beowulf in the round, before forming an opinion about this. What seems more likely to me is that the poet was voicing some reservations about the heroic code, which induced a king to fight single-handed against a dragon, motivated by intense desire for glory, and thereby imperil his people. Perhaps there is a hint that, in the end, the old heroic ideal does not measure up to the new Christian ideal.

But I do not believe for one moment that this reservation is the main purpose of the poem. Whichever interpretation you choose, it is impossible to overlook the overwhelmingly positive tone of *Beowulf*. Its main purpose may or may not be to portray the transitoriness of human life, the rise and fall of empires, the similarity or disparity of the pagan ethos and Christian ideal, the glory or the shortcomings of the old heroic code, but the warp and weft of the poem proclaim the importance of kinship and loyalty, and physical and moral courage; they gleam with images of drinking, feasting, the swearing of friendship, and the giving of gold; they assert the value of life. *Beowulf* is a celebration, not a motion of censure.

There are not many great long poems in the world, and few of us are accustomed to reading them. We are more likely to turn to prose fiction than to poetry and,

if we do read poetry, more likely to read lyric poems, short by definition, than the work of Virgil or Milton or even Wordsworth. So a few comments on the practical business of approaching and reading *Beowulf* may not be out of place.

Beowulf, like all Anglo-Saxon poetry, was first intended to be *heard*. For this reason, its movement is stately, even slow. Its characteristic movement is rather like that of a crab, one step forwards, one step sideways. The poet says, for instance, 'flota waes on yðum, bat under beorge' which literally means 'floater was on waves, boat under cliff'. These two clauses have one idea in common – the boat – while the second clause introduces a new idea: the cliff. One of the purposes of this parallelism must surely have been to allow the audience time to digest the story.

One way round the fact that the poem was designed to be heard and yet is here presented on the page is quite simply to voice it as you read it – to say the words to yourself or, even better, to share them. However well developed your inner ear, your perception of the poem is likely to change and develop if you try this method.

Partly because *Beowulf* is a long poem, perhaps originally recited over a period of three evenings, the poet does not rush into the action. He calmly sets the scene; he establishes the lineage of the Danish royal house; he alludes to kings, queens and princes who are never mentioned again. So my second simple recommendation is that, if you are coming to this poem for the first time, you should gallop through the first one hundred lines and get into the

The Anglo-Saxons produced jewellery of outstanding quality. This detail from a ring illustrates the high level of craftsmanship with fine strands of gold delicately interwoven like thread.

story proper. I can think of a dozen great works of literature that have 'difficult' beginnings and *Beowulf* is one of them.

So much for the text of *Beowulf*. This wonderful poem belongs to the Northern World and there is one further step that will enable you to 'read' it. On site or in museum or in book, look at the fantastic array of buildings and artefacts that survive from the Dark Ages. The interlace design so characteristic of manuscript border and jewellery decoration is a useful analogy to *Beowulf*'s highly wrought versification; the dragon on the Sutton Hoo shield, a terrifying creature with a blood garnet eye, brings home the ferocity – even the animality – of Anglo-Saxon warfare; the ninth-century gravestone, with Norse axemen rampant on one side and on the other two monks bowed in prayer, illustrates the abiding and touching piety of the Anglo-Saxon Christianity – a devoted and steadfast gaze in the teeth of terror and darkness.

Some awareness of the cultural achievement of the Germanic-speaking peoples of Dark Age Europe can only quicken one's appreciation of its greatest literary cornerstone, *Beowulf*. But the reverse is also true. A reading of the poem is not only satisfying as an imaginative experience in itself and an inimitable way of grasping what it was like to live in England perhaps thirteen hundred years ago; it is also a powerful stimulus. The curious reader will step beyond the poem, 'isig ond ut-fus', as the *Beowulf*-poet says, 'icy and out-eager'; he or she will want to set the poem in a wider artistic and social context and will discover, as our wise poet knows, 'many a fine sight for those with eyes for such things'.

THE WORLD OF *BEOWULF*

The Beowulf poem was written in Britain, but the events it relates occur in what is now Denmark and Sweden. The map illustrates the rough position of the various kingdoms and the relative distances between them.

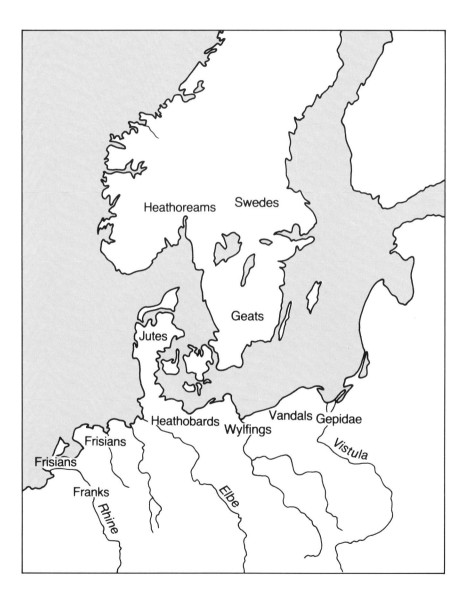

GENEALOGICAL TABLES

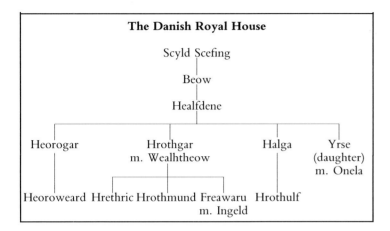

The Danish Royal House

Scyld Scefing

Beow

Healfdene

Heorogar   Hrothgar   Halga   Yrse
         m. Wealhtheow   (daughter)
                             m. Onela

Heoroweard   Hrethric   Hrothmund   Freawaru   Hrothulf
                               m. Ingeld

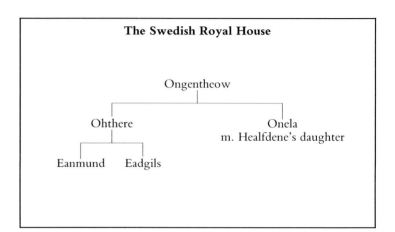

The Swedish Royal House

Ongentheow

Ohthere   Onela
                m. Healfdene's daughter

Eanmund   Eadgils

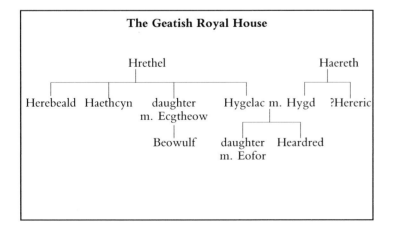

The Geatish Royal House

Hrethel   Haereth

Herebeald   Haethcyn   daughter   Hygelac m. Hygd   ?Hereric
                       m. Ecgtheow

          Beowulf   daughter   Heardred
                       m. Eofor

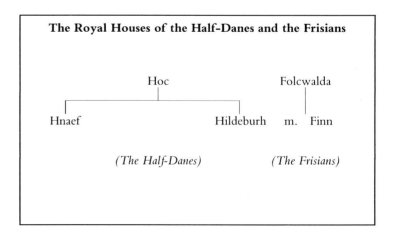

The Royal Houses of the Half-Danes and the Frisians

Hoc   Folcwalda

Hnaef   Hildeburh   m.   Finn

(The Half-Danes)   *(The Frisians)*

WHO'S WHO

A glossary of proper names and place names

Ælfhere   King of the Danes; member of the Waegmunding family.

Æschere   Old Danish warrior carried off and killed by Grendel's mother.

Beanstan   A Bronding warrior. The father of Breca, Beowulf's swimming rival.

Beow   King of the Danes; son of Scyld Scefing.

Beowulf   A Geat. His father was Ecgtheow and his mother was sister to King Hygelac. Hero of the poem.

Breca   A Bronding warrior. Beowulf's swimming rival.

Brondings   The tribe to which Beanstan and Breca belong.

Brosings   A family or race of dwarfs. The legendary necklace (or possibly belt) of the Brosings (or Brisings) was first given to the goddess Freyja by four dwarfs in return for her favours.

Cain   Son of Adam and Eve, and murderer of his brother Abel.

Dæghrefn   The greatest of Frisian warriors. He was killed by Beowulf.

Danes   Inhabitants of Denmark. They are also referred to as Scyldings, Ring-Danes, Spear-Danes, North-Danes, South-Danes, East-Danes and West-Danes.

Eadgils   Swedish prince; the son of Ohthere. He seeks help at the Geatish court of Heardred.

Eanmund   Swedish prince; the son of Ohthere. He was one-time owner of the sword that passed to Wiglaf.

Ecglaf   Father of Unferth, the Danish warrior who taunts Beowulf.

Ecgtheow   Beowulf's father.

Ecgwala   King of the Danes.

Eofor   Geatish warrior. Son of Wonred. He killed Ongentheow and was given Hygelac's daughter in marriage as a reward.

Eomer   Son of Offa, fourth-century king of the Angles.

Eormenric	Ermanaric, king of the East Goths in the fourth century; a tyrant.
Finn	King of the Frisians.
Fitela	Nephew of the dragon-slayer, Sigemund.
Folcwalda	Finn's father.
Franks	A people living in the eastern Netherlands on and around the Rhine.
Freawaru	Danish princess; Hrothgar's daughter. She married Ingeld.
Frisia	Home of the Frisians. Present-day Friesland, Noord Holland and Zuid Holland in the Netherlands.
Froda	King of the Heathobards, a tribe living in northern Germany. Father of Ingeld.
Garmund	Father of Hygelac; grandfather of Eomer.
Geats	A tribe living in the south-west of Sweden. They are also referred to as the Storm-Geats.
Gepidae	A tribe living around the Gulf of Danzig in Poland.
Grendel	A monster, descended from Cain. He and Beowulf fight hand to hand in Heorot.
Guthlaf	A Half-Dane warrior.
Hæreth	Father of Hygd, queen of the Geats.
Hæthcyn	Geatish prince; son of Hrethel. He accidentally killed his elder brother Herebeald. He was killed in battle at Ravenswood by Ongentheow.
Half-Danes	The Danes who were followers of Hnaef and then Hengest.
Halga	Danish prince; great-grandson of Scyld Scefing.
Hama	Owner of the necklace of the Brosings (see Brosings).
Healfdene	King of the Danes; son of Beow, grandson of Scyld Scefing, and father of Hrothgar.
Heardred	King of the Geats; son of Hygelac. He was killed by Onela after receiving at his court and helping Onela's rebellious nephews.
Heathobards	A tribe living between Bremen and Lübeck in northern Germany.
Heatholaf	A warrior of the Wylfing tribe slain by Ecgtheow, Beowulf's father.
Heathoreams	A tribe living around Oslo in the south-east of Norway.

Helmings	The family of which Wealtheow is a member.
Hemming	Kinsman of King Offa.
Hengest	The leader of the Half-Danes after the death of Hnaef. He is probably the same Hengest who with Horsa came to England in AD 449 at the invitation of Vortigern, and later founded the Anglo-Saxon kingdom of Kent.
Heorogar	King of the Danes; son of Healfdene and great-grandson of Scyld Scefing.
Heorot	The feasting-hall built by Hrothgar, king of the Danes.
Heoroweard	Danish prince; son of Hrothgar.
Herebeald	Geatish prince; eldest son of Hrethel. He was accidentally killed by his younger brother Haethcyn.
Heremod	King of Denmark immediately before Scyld.
Hereric	Uncle of Heardred, king of the Geats. He was probably the brother of Queen Hygd.
Hildeburh	Danish princess; sister of Hnaef and wife of Finn, king of the Frisians.
Hnæf	Leader of Half-Danes, who was killed by Finn, king of the Frisians.
Hoc	Hildeburh's father.
Hondscio	Geatish warrior ripped apart and eaten by Grendel.
Hrethel	King of the Geats; father of Hygelac. His only daughter married Ecgtheow, Beowulf's father.
Hrethric	Danish prince; son of Hrothgar and Wealhtheow.
Hrothgar	King of Denmark; son of Healfdene and great-grandson of Scyld Scefing.
Hrothmund	Danish prince; son of Hrothgar and Wealhtheow.
Hrothulf	Danish prince; nephew to Hrothgar. After Hrothgar's death, he kills Hrothgar's son Hrethric.
Hrunting	A sword lent by Unferth to Beowulf.
Hunlafing	Half-Dane warrior serving under Hengest.
Hygd	Queen of the Geats; wife of Hygelac.

Hygelac	King of the Geats; son of Hrethel. Beowulf was his sister's son. He was killed in Frisia by the Franks.
Ing	Early king and possibly god of the Danes.
Ingeld	King of the Heathobards. Son of Froda and affianced to Freawaru, the daughter of Hrothgar.
Jutes	A tribe (also referred to as the East Frisians) living in Jylland (or Jutland) in northern Denmark.
Lapps	A tribe living in northern Sweden and Norway.
Nægling	Beowulf's sword. It snapped in the skull of the dragon.
Offa	King of the Angles who married and tamed Thryth.
Ohthere	Swedish prince. Son of Ongentheow.
Onela	King of Sweden. Son of Ongentheow. He married Healfdene's daughter and was killed by Eadgils.
Ongentheow	King of the Swedes. He was slain by Eofor shortly after the battle at Ravenswood.
Oslaf	Half-Dane warrior.
Ravenswood	Site of a battle between the Geats and the Swedes.
Scyld Scefing	Legendary Danish king from whom the Scyldings (descendants of Scyld) take their name.
Scyldings	Danes.
Sigemund	Legendary dragon-slayer and one of the most famous of Northern heroes.
Slaughter Hill	Site of several battles in which the sons of Ongentheow butchered the Geats.
Swedes	A tribe living in central Sweden.
Swerting	A Geatish warrior. Either the uncle or grandfather of Hygelac.
Thryth	(Possibly Modthryth) An arrogant queen unfavourably compared with Hygd.
Unferth	Danish warrior. Son of Ecglaf. He taunts Beowulf while in his cups, and later lends him his sword Hrunting.
Vandals	A tribe living between Szczecin and Gdansk in northern Poland.
Wægmundings	Family to whom both Beowulf and Wiglaf belonged.

Wæls	Sigemund's father.
Wealhtheow	Queen of the Geats; wife of Hrothgar.
Weland	The master-smith of Germanic legend.
Weohstan	A member of the Waegmunding family. Father of Wiglaf and slayer of the Swede Eanmund.
Whaleness	Headland overlooking the sea; the site of Beowulf's barrow.
Wiglaf	Swedish prince. A kinsman of Beowulf and member of the Waegmunding family. He helped Beowulf to fight against the dragon.
Withergyld	Heathobard warrior slain in battle by the Scyldings.
Wonred	Geatish warrior. Father of Wulf.
Wulf	Geatish warrior. Son of Wonred and brother of Eofor. He was wounded by Ongentheow.
Wulfgar	Prince of the Vandals. He served at Hrothgar's court.
Wylfings	A tribe living around Gdansk in Poland. Beowulf's father, Ecgtheow, began a feud by killing Heatholaf of the Wylfings; and Hrothgar settled it by payment of *wergild*.
Yrmenlaf	Æschere's younger brother.
Yrse	Danish princess; daughter of Healfdene and great-granddaughter of Scyld Scefing. She married Onela, king of Sweden.

Beowulf

THE POEM

Listen!
      The fame of Danish kings
in days gone by, the daring feats
worked by those heroes are well known to us.
    Scyld Scefing often deprived his enemies,
many tribes of men, of their mead-benches.
He terrified his foes; yet he, as a boy,
had been found a waif; fate made amends for that.
He prospered under heaven, won praise and honour
until the men of every neighbouring tribe,
across the whale's way, were obliged to obey him
and pay him tribute. He was a noble king!
Then a son was born to him, a child
in the court, sent by God to comfort
the Danes; for He had seen their dire distress,
that once they suffered hardship for a long while,
lacking a lord; and the Lord of Life,
King of Heaven, granted this boy glory;
Beow was renowned – the name of Scyld's son
became known throughout the Norse lands.
By his own mettle, likewise by generous gifts
while he still enjoys his father's protection,
a young man must ensure that in later years

his companions will support him, serve
their prince in battle; a man who wins renown
will always prosper among any people.
    Then Scyld departed at the destined hour,
that powerful man sought the Lord's protection.
His own close companions carried him
down to the sea, as he, lord of the Danes,
had asked while he could still speak.
That well-loved man had ruled his land for many years.
There in harbour stood the ring-prowed ship,
the prince's vessel, icy, eager to sail;
and then they laid their dear lord,
the giver of rings, deep within the ship
by the mast in majesty; many treasures
and adornments from far and wide were gathered there.
I have never heard of a ship equipped
more handsomely with weapons and war-gear,
swords and corslets; on his breast
lay countless treasures that were to travel far
with him into the waves' domain.
They gave him great ornaments, gifts
no less magnificent than those men had given him
who long before had sent him alone,

child as he was, across the stretch of the seas.
Then high above his head they placed
a golden banner and let the waves bear him,
bequeathed him to the sea; their hearts were grieving,
their minds mourning. Mighty men
beneath the heavens, rulers in the hall,
cannot say who received that cargo.

When his royal father had travelled from the earth,
Beow of Denmark, a beloved king,
ruled long in the stronghold, famed
amongst men; in time Healfdene the brave
was born to him; who, so long as he lived,
grey-haired and redoubtable, ruled the noble Danes.
Beow's son Healfdene, leader of men,
was favoured by fortune with four children:
Heorogar and Hrothgar and Halga the good;
Yrse, the fourth, was Onela's queen,
the dear wife of that warlike Swedish king.

Hrothgar won honour in war,
glory in battle, and so ensured
his followers' support — young men
whose number multiplied into a mighty troop.
And he resolved to build a hall,

a large and noble feasting-hall
of whose splendours men would always speak,
and there to distribute as gifts to old and young
all the things that God had given him —
but not men's lives or the public land.
Then I heard that tribes without number, even
to the ends of the earth, were given orders
to decorate the hall. And in due course
(before very long) this greatest of halls
was completed. Hrothgar, whose very word was counted
far and wide as a command, called it Heorot.
He kept his promise, gave presents of rings
and treasure at the feasting. The hall towered high,
lofty and wide-gabled — fierce tongues of loathsome fire
had not yet attacked it, nor was the time yet near
when a mortal feud should flare between father-
and son-in-law, sparked off by deeds of deadly enmity.
    Then the brutish demon who lived in darkness
impatiently endured a time of frustration:
day after day he heard the din of merry-making
inside the hall, and the sound of the harp
and the bard's clear song. He who could tell
of the origin of men from far-off times lifted his voice,

sang that the Almighty made the earth,
this radiant plain encompassed by oceans;
and that God, all powerful, ordained
sun and moon to shine for mankind,
adorned all regions of the world
with trees and leaves; and sang that He gave life
to every kind of creature that walks about earth.
So those warrior Danes lived joyful lives,
in complete harmony, until the hellish fiend
began to perpetrate base crimes.
This gruesome creature was called Grendel,
notorious prowler of the borderland, ranger of the moors,
the fen and the fastness; this cursed creature
lived in a monster's lair for a time
after the Creator had condemned him
as one of the seed of Cain — the Everlasting Lord
avenged Abel's murder. Cain had
no satisfaction from that feud, but the Creator
sent him into exile, far from mankind,
because of his crime. He could no longer
approach the throne of grace, that precious place
in God's presence, nor did he feel God's love.
In him all evil-doers find their origin,

monsters and elves and spiteful spirits of the dead,
also the giants who grappled with God
for a long while; the Lord gave them their deserts.
    Then, under cover of night, Grendel came
to Hrothgar's lofty hall to see how the Ring-Danes
were disposed after drinking ale all evening;
and he found there a band of brave warriors,
well-feasted, fast asleep, dead to worldly sorrow,
man's sad destiny. At once that hellish monster,
grim and greedy, brutally cruel,
started forward and seized thirty thanes
even as they slept; and then, gloating
over his plunder, he hurried from the hall,
made for his lair with all those slain warriors.
Then at dawn, as day first broke,
Grendel's power was at once revealed;
a great lament was lifted, after the feast
an anguished cry at that daylight discovery.
The famous prince, best of all men, sat apart in
    mourning;
when he saw Grendel's gruesome footprints,
that great man grieved for his retainers.
This enmity was utterly one-sided, too repulsive,

too long-lasting. Nor were the Danes allowed respite,
but the very next day Grendel committed
violent assault, murders more atrocious than before,
and he had no qualms about it. He was caught up in his
    crimes.
Then it was not difficult to find the man
who preferred a more distant resting-place,
a bed in the outbuildings, for the hatred
of the hall-warden was quite unmistakable.
He who had escaped the clutches of the fiend
kept further off, at a safe distance.
    Thus Grendel ruled, resisted justice,
one against all, until the best of halls
stood deserted. And so it remained:
for twelve long winters the lord of the Danes
was sorely afflicted with sorrows and cares;
then men were reminded in mournful songs
that the monster Grendel fought with Hrothgar
for a long time, fought with fierce hatred
committing crime and atrocity day after day
in continual strife. He had no wish for peace
with any of the Danes, would not desist
from his deadly malice or pay *wergild* —

No! None of the counsellors could hold out hope
of handsome compensation at that slayer's hands.
But the cruel monster constantly terrified
young and old, the dark death-shadow
lurked in ambush; he prowled the misty moors
at the dead of night; men do not know
where such hell-whisperers shrithe in their wanderings.
Such were the many and outrageous injuries
that the fearful solitary, foe of all men,
endlessly inflicted; he occupied Heorot,
that hall adorned with treasures, on cloudless nights.
This caused the lord of the Danes deep,
heart-breaking grief. Strong men often sat
in consultation, trying in vain to devise
a good plan as to how best valiant men
could safeguard themselves against sudden attack.
At times they offered sacrifices to the idols
in their pagan tabernacles, and prayed aloud
to the soul-slayer that he would assist them
in their dire distress. Such was the custom
and comfort of the heathen; they brooded in their hearts
on hellish things — for the Creator, Almighty God,
the judge of all actions, was neglected by them;

truly they did not know how to praise the Protector of
    Heaven,
the glorious Ruler. Woe to the man who,
in his wickedness, commits his soul to the fire's embrace;
he must expect neither comfort nor change.
He will be damned for ever. Joy shall be his
who, when he dies, may stand before the Lord,
seek peace in the embrace of our Father.

   Thus Healfdene's son endlessly brooded
over the afflictions of this time; that wise warrior
was altogether helpless, for the hardship upon them –
violent visitations, evil events in the night –
was too overwhelming, loathsome, and long-lasting.

   One of Hygelac's thanes, Beowulf by name,
renowned among the Geats for his great bravery,
heard in his own country of Grendel's crimes;
he was the strongest man alive,
princely and powerful. He gave orders
that a good ship should be prepared, said he would sail
over the sea to assist the famous leader,
the warrior king, since he needed hardy men.
Wise men admired his spirit of adventure.
Dear to them though he was, they encouraged

the warrior and consulted the omens.
Beowulf searched out the bravest of the Geats,
asked them to go with him; that seasoned sailor
led fourteen thanes to the ship at the shore.
    Days went by; the boat was on the water,
moored under the cliff. The warriors, all prepared,
stepped onto the prow – the water streams eddied,
stirred up sand; the men stowed
gleaming armour, noble war-gear
deep within the ship; then those warriors launched
the well-built boat and so began their journey.
Foaming at the prow and most like a sea-bird,
the boat sped over the waves, urged on by the wind;
until next day, at about the expected time,
so far had the curved prow come
that the travellers sighted land,
shining cliffs, steep hills,
broad headlands. So did they cross the sea;
their journey was at its end. Then the Geats
disembarked, lost no time in tying up
the boat – their corslets clanked;
the warriors gave thanks to God
for their safe passage over the sea.

Then, on the cliff-top, the Danish watchman
(whose duty it was to stand guard by the shore)
saw that the Geats carried flashing shields
and gleaming war-gear down the gangway,
and his mind was riddled with curiosity.
Then Hrothgar's thane leaped onto his horse
and, brandishing a spear, galloped
down to the shore; there, he asked at once:
'Warriors! Who are you, in your coats of mail,
who have steered your tall ship over the sea-lanes
to these shores? I've been a coastguard here
for many years, kept watch by the sea,
so that no enemy band should encroach
upon this Danish land and do us injury.
Never have warriors, carrying their shields,
come to this country in a more open manner.
Nor were you assured of my leaders' approval,
my kinsmen's consent. I've never set eyes
on a more noble man, a warrior in armour,
than one among your band; he's no mere retainer,
so ennobled by his weapons. May his looks never belie
    him,
and his lordly bearing. But now, before you step

one foot further on Danish land
like faithless spies, I must know
your lineage. Bold seafarers,
strangers from afar, mark my words
carefully: you would be best advised
quickly to tell me the cause of your coming.'
    The man of highest standing, leader of that troop,
unlocked his hoard of words, answered him:
'We are all Geats, hearth-companions of Hygelac;
my father was famed far and wide,
a noble lord! Ecgtheow by name —
he endured many winters before he,
in great old age, went on his way; every wise man
in this world readily recalls him.
We have sailed across the sea to seek your lord,
Healfdene's son, protector of the people,
with most honourable intentions; give us your guidance!
We have come on an errand of importance
to the great Danish prince; nor, I imagine, will the cause
of our coming long remain secret. You will know
whether it is true — as we have heard tell —
that here among the Danes a certain evil-doer,
a fearful solitary, on dark nights commits deeds

of unspeakable malice – damage
and slaughter. In good conscience
I can counsel Hrothgar, that wise and good man,
how he shall overcome the fiend,
and how his anguish shall be assuaged –
if indeed his fate ordains that these foul deeds
should ever end, and be avenged;
he will suffer endless hardship otherwise,
dire distress, as long as Heorot, best of dwellings,
stands unshaken in its lofty place.'

    Still mounted, the coastguard,
a courageous thane, gave him this reply:
'The discriminating warrior – one whose mind is keen –
must perceive the difference between words and deeds.
But I see you are a company well disposed
towards the Danish prince. Proceed, and bring
your weapons and armour! I shall direct you.
And I will command my companions, moreover,
to guard your ship with honour
against any foe – your beached vessel,
caulked so recently – until the day that timbered craft
with its curved prow shall carry back
the beloved man across the sea currents

to the shores of the storm-loving Geats:
he who dares deeds with such audacity and valour
shall be granted safety in the squall of battle.'

    Then they hurried on. The ship lay still;
securely anchored, the spacious vessel
rode on its hawser. The boar crest, brightly gleaming,
stood over their helmets: superbly tempered,
plated with glowing gold, it guarded the lives
of those grim warriors. The thanes made haste,
marched along together until they could discern
the glorious, timbered hall, adorned with gold;
they saw there the best-known building
under heaven. The ruler lived in it;
its brilliance carried across countless lands.
Then the fearless watchman pointed out the path
leading to Heorot, bright home of brave men,
so that they should not miss the way;
that bold warrior turned his horse, then said:
'I must leave you here. May the Almighty Father,
of His grace, guard you in your enterprise.
I will go back to the sea again,
and there stand watch against marauding bands.'

    The road was paved; it showed those warriors

the way. Their corslets were gleaming,
the strong links of shining chain-mail
clinked together. When the sea-stained travellers
had reached the hall itself in their fearsome armour,
they placed their broad shields
(worked so skilfully) against Heorot's wall.
Then they sat on a bench; the brave men's
armour sang. The seafarers' gear
stood all together, a grey-tipped forest
of ash spears; that armed troop was well equipped
with weapons.
        Then Wulfgar, a proud warrior,
asked the Geats about their ancestry:
'Where have you come from with these gold-plated
    shields,
these grey coats of mail, these visored helmets,
and this pile of spears? I am Hrothgar's
messenger, his herald, I have never seen
so large a band of strangers of such bold bearing.
You must have come to Hrothgar's court
not as exiles, but from audacity and high ambition.'
Then he who feared no man, the proud leader
of the Geats, stern-faced beneath his helmet,

gave him this reply: 'We are Hygelac's
companions at the bench: my name is Beowulf.
I wish to explain to Healfdene's son,
the famous prince, your lord,
why we have come if he, in his goodness,
will give us leave to speak with him.'
Wulfgar replied – a prince of the Vandals,
his mettle, his wisdom and prowess in battle
were widely recognized: 'I will ask
the lord of the Danes, ruler of the Scyldings,
renowned prince and ring-giver,
just as you request, regarding your journey,
and bring back to you at once whatever answer
that gracious man thinks fit to give me.'
    Then Wulfgar hurried to the place where
                        Hrothgar sat,
grizzled and old, surrounded by his thanes;
the brave man moved forward until he stood
immediately before the Danish lord;
he well knew the customs of warriors.
Wulfgar addressed his friend and leader:
'Geatish men have travelled to this land,
come from far, across the stretch of the seas.

These warriors call their leader Beowulf;
they ask, my lord, that they should be allowed
to speak with you. Gracious Hrothgar,
do not give them *no* for answer.
They, in their armour, seem altogether worthy
of the highest esteem. I have no doubt of their leader's
might, he who has brought these brave men to Heorot.'
Hrothgar, defender of the Danes, answered:
'I knew him when he was a boy;
his illustrious father was called Ecgtheow;
Hrethel the Geat gave him his only daughter
in marriage; now his son, with daring spirit,
has voyaged here to visit a loyal friend.
And moreover, I have heard seafarers say –
men who have carried rich gifts to the Geats
as a mark of my esteem – that in the grasp
of his hand that man renowned in battle
has the might of thirty men. I am convinced
that Holy God, of His great mercy,
has directed him to us West-Danes
and that he means to come to grips with Grendel.
I will reward this brave man with treasures.
Hurry! Tell them to come in and meet

our band of kinsmen; and make it clear, too,
that they are most welcome to the Danes!'
Then Wulfgar went to the hall door with Hrothgar's
    reply:
'My conquering lord, the leader of the East-Danes
commands me to tell you that he knows your lineage
and that you, so bold in mind, are welcome
to these shores from over the rolling sea.
You may see Hrothgar in your armour,
under your helmets, just as you are;
but leave your shields out here, and your deadly ashen
    spears,
let them await the outcome of your words.'
    Then noble Beowulf rose from the bench,
flanked by his fearless followers; some stayed behind
at the brave man's bidding, to stand guard over their
    armour.
Guided by Wulfgar, the rest hurried into Heorot
together; there went that hardy man, stern-faced
beneath his helmet, until he was standing under Heorot's
    roof.
Beowulf spoke — his corslet, cunningly linked
by the smith, was shining: 'Greetings, Hrothgar!

I am Hygelac's kinsman and retainer. In my youth
I achieved many daring exploits. Word of Grendel's deeds
has come to me in my own country;
seafarers say that this hall Heorot,
best of all buildings, stands empty and useless
as soon as the evening light is hidden under the sky.
So, Lord Hrothgar, men known by my people
to be noble and wise advised me to visit you
because they knew of my great strength:
they saw me themselves when, stained by my enemies'
    blood,
I returned from the fight when I destroyed five,
a family of giants, and by night slew monsters
on the waves; I suffered great hardship,
avenged the affliction of the Storm-Geats and crushed
their fierce foes — they were asking for trouble.
And now, I shall crush the giant Grendel
in single combat. Lord of the mighty Danes,
guardian of the Scyldings, I ask one favour:
protector of warriors, lord beloved of your people,
now that I have sailed here from so far,
do not refuse my request — that I alone, with my band
of brave retainers, may cleanse Heorot.

I have also heard men say this monster
is so reckless he spurns the use of weapons.
Therefore (so that Hygelac, my lord,
may rest content over my conduct) I deny myself
the use of a sword and a broad yellow shield
in battle; but I shall grapple with this fiend
hand to hand; we shall fight for our lives,
foe against foe; and he whom death takes off
must resign himself to the judgement of God.
I know that Grendel, should he overcome me,
will without dread devour many Geats,
matchless warriors, in the battle-hall,
as he has often devoured Danes before. If death claims me
you will not have to cover my head,
for he already will have done so —
with a sheet of shining blood; he will carry off
the blood-stained corpse, meaning to savour it;
the solitary one will eat without sorrow
and stain his lair; no longer then
will you have to worry about burying my body.
But if battle should claim me, send this most excellent
coat of mail to Hygelac, this best of corslets
that protects my breast; it belonged to Hrethel,

the work of Weland. Fate goes ever as it must!'
    Hrothgar, protector of the Scyldings, replied:
'Beowulf, my friend! So you have come here,
because of past favours, to fight on our behalf!
Your father Ecgtheow, by striking a blow,
began the greatest of feuds. He slew Heatholaf of the
    Wylfings
with his own hand; after that, the Geats
dared not harbour him for fear of war.
So he sailed here, over the rolling waves,
to this land of the South-Danes, the honoured Scyldings;
I was young then, had just begun to reign
over the Danes in this glorious kingdom,
this treasure-stronghold of heroes; my elder brother,
Heorogar, Healfdene's son, had died
not long before; he was a better man than I!
I settled your father's feud by payment;
I sent ancient treasures to the Wylfings
over the water's back; and Ecgtheow swore oaths to me.
It fills me with anguish to admit to all the evil
that Grendel, goaded on by his hatred,
has wreaked in Heorot with his sudden attacks
and infliction of injuries; my hall-troop is depleted

my band of warriors; fate has swept them
into Grendel's ghastly clutches. Yet God can easily
prevent this reckless ravager from committing such crimes.
After quaffing beer, brave warriors of mine
have often boasted over the ale-cup
that they would wait in Heorot
and fight against Grendel with their fearsome swords.
Then, the next morning, when day dawned,
men could see that this great mead-hall was stained
by blood, that the floor by the benches
was spattered with gore; I had fewer followers,
dear warriors, for death had taken them off.
But first, sit down at our feast, and in due course,
as your inclination takes you, tell how warriors
have achieved greatness.'
              Then, in the feasting-hall,
a bench was cleared for the Geats all together,
and there those brave men went and sat,
delighting in their strength; a thane did his duty —
held between his hands the adorned ale-cup,
poured out gleaming liquor; now and then the poet
raised his voice, resonant in Heorot; the warriors
   caroused,

no small company of Scyldings and Geats.
Ecglaf's son, Unferth, who sat at the feet
of the lord of the Scyldings, unlocked his thoughts
with these unfriendly words — for the journey of Beowulf,
the brave seafarer, much displeased him
in that he was unwilling for any man
in this wide world to gain more glory than himself:
'Are you the Beowulf who competed with Breca,
vied with him at swimming in the open sea
when, swollen with vanity, you both braved
the waves, risked your lives on deep waters
because of a foolish boast? No one,
neither friend nor foe, could keep you
from your sad journey, when you swam out to sea,
clasped in your arms the water-streams,
passed over the sea-paths, swiftly moved your hands
and sped over the ocean. The sea heaved,
the winter flood; for seven nights
you both toiled in the water; but Breca outstayed you,
he was the stronger; and then, on the eighth morning,
the sea washed him up on the shores of the
   Heathoreams.
From there he sought his own country,

the land of the Brondings who loved him well;
he went to his fair stronghold where he had a hall
and followers and treasures. In truth, Beanstan's son
fulfilled his boast that he could swim better than you.
So I am sure you will pay a heavy price —
although you have survived countless battle storms,
savage sword-play — if you dare
ambush Grendel in the watches of the night.'
Beowulf, the son of Ecgtheow, replied:
'Truly, Unferth my friend, all this beer
has made you talkative: you have told us much
about Breca and his exploits. But I maintain
I showed the greater stamina, endured
hardship without equal in the heaving water.
Some years ago when we were young men,
still in our youth, Breca and I made a boast,
a solemn vow, to venture our lives
on the open sea; and we kept our word.
When we swam through the water, we each held
a naked sword with which to ward off
whales; by no means could Breca
swim faster than I, pull away from me
through the press of the waves —

I had no wish to be separated from him.
So for five nights we stayed together in the sea,
until the tides tore us apart,
the foaming water, the freezing cold,
day darkening into night — until the north wind,
that savage warrior, rounded against us.
Rough were the waves; fishes in the sea
were roused to great anger. Then my coat of mail,
hard and hand-linked, guarded me against my enemies;
the woven war-garment, adorned with gold,
covered my breast. A cruel ravager
dragged me down to the sea-bed, a fierce monster
held me tightly in its grasp; but it was given to me
to bury my sword, my battle weapon,
in its breast; the mighty sea-beast
was slain by my blow in the storm of battle.
In this manner, and many times, loathsome monsters
harassed me fiercely; with my fine sword
I served them fittingly.
I did not allow those evil destroyers to enjoy
a feast, to eat me limb by limb
seated at a banquet on the sea-bottom;
but the next morning they lay in the sand

along the shore, wounded by sword strokes,
slain by battle-blades, and from that day on
they could not hinder seafarers from sailing
over deep waters. Light came from the east,
God's bright beacon; the swell subsided,
and I saw then great headlands,
cliffs swept by the wind. Fate will often spare
an undoomed man, if his courage is good.
As it was I slew nine sea-beasts
with my sword. I have never heard
of a fiercer fight by night under heaven's vault
nor of a man who endured more on the ocean streams.
But I escaped with my life from the enemies' clutches,
worn out by my venture. Then the swift current,
the surging water, carried me
to the land of the Lapps. I have not heard tell
that you have taken part in any such contests,
in the peril of sword-play. Neither you nor Breca
have yet dared such a deed with shining sword
in battle — I do not boast because of this —
though of course it is true you slew your own brothers,
your own close kinsmen. For that deed, however clever
you may be, you will suffer damnation in hell.

I tell you truly, son of Ecglaf,
that if you were in fact as unflinching
as you claim, the fearsome monster Grendel
would never have committed so many crimes
against your lord, nor created such havoc in Heorot;
but he has found he need not fear unduly
your people's enmity, fearsome assault
with swords by the victorious Scyldings.
So he spares none but takes his toll
of the Danish people, does as he will,
kills and destroys, expects no fight
from the Spear-Danes. But soon, quite soon,
I shall show him the strength, the spirit and skill
of the Geats. And thereafter, when day dawns,
when the radiant sun shines from the south
over the sons of men, he who so wishes
may enter the mead-hall without terror.'

Then the grizzled warrior, giver of gold,
was filled with joy; the lord of the Danes,
shepherd of his people, listened to Beowulf's
brave resolution and relied on his help.
The warriors laughed, there was a hum
of contentment. Wealhtheow came forward,

mindful of ceremonial – she was Hrothgar's queen;
adorned with gold, that proud woman
greeted the men in the hall, then offered the cup
to the Danish king first of all.
She begged him, beloved of his people,
to enjoy the feast; the king, famed
for victory, ate and drank in happiness.
Then the lady of the Helmings walked about the hall,
offering the precious, ornamented cup
to old and young alike, until at last
the queen, excellent in mind, adorned with rings,
moved with the mead-cup towards Beowulf.
She welcomed the Geatish prince and with wise words
thanked God that her wish was granted
that she might depend on some warrior for help
against such attacks. The courageous man
took the cup from Wealhtheow's hands
and, eager for battle, made a speech:
Beowulf, the son of Ecgtheow, said:
'When I put to sea, sailed
through the breakers with my band of men,
I resolved to fulfil the desire
of your people, or suffer the pangs of death,

caught fast in Grendel's clutches.
Here, in Heorot, I shall either work a deed
of great daring, or lay down my life.'
Beowulf's brave boast delighted Wealhtheow:
adorned with gold, the noble Danish queen
went to sit beside her lord.
    Then again, as of old, fine words were spoken
in the hall, the company rejoiced,
a conquering people, until in due course
the son of Healfdene wanted to retire
and take his rest. He realized the monster
meant to attack Heorot after the blue hour,
when black night has settled over all –
when shadowy shapes come shrithing
dark beneath the clouds. All the company rose.
Then the heroes Hrothgar and Beowulf saluted
one another; Hrothgar wished him luck
and control of Heorot, and confessed:
'Never since I could lift hand and shield,
have I entrusted this glorious Danish hall
to any man as I do now to you.
Take and guard this greatest of halls.
Make known your strength, remember your might,

stand watch against your enemy. You shall have
all you desire if you survive this enterprise.'
  Then Hrothgar, defender of the Danes,
withdrew from the hall with his band of warriors.
The warlike leader wanted to sleep with Wealhtheow,
his queen. It was said the mighty king
had appointed a hall-guard – a man who undertook
a dangerous duty for the Danish king,
elected to stand watch against the monster.
Truly, the leader of the Geats fervently trusted
in his own great strength and in God's grace.
Then he took off his helmet and his corslet
of iron, and gave them to his servant,
with his superb, adorned sword,
telling him to guard them carefully.
And then, before he went to his bed,
the brave Geat, Beowulf, made his boast:
'I count myself no less active in battle,
no less brave than Grendel himself:
thus, I will not send him to sleep with my sword,
so deprive him of life, though certainly I could.
Despite his fame for deadly deeds,
he is ignorant of these noble arts, that he might strike

at me, and hew my shield; but we, this night,
shall forego the use of weapons, if he dares fight
without them; and then may wise God,
the holy Lord, give glory in battle
to whichever of us He should think fitting.'
Then the brave prince leaned back, put his head
on the pillow while, around him,
many a proud seafarer lay back on his bed.
Not one of them believed he would see
day dawn, or ever return to his family
and friends, and the place where he was born;
they well knew that in recent days
far too many Danish men had come to bloody ends
in that hall. But the Lord wove the webs of destiny,
gave the Geats success in their struggle,
help and support, in such a way
that all were enabled to overcome their enemy
through the strength of one man. We cannot doubt
that mighty God has always ruled
over mankind.
           Then the night prowler
came shrithing through the shadows. All the Geats
guarding Heorot had fallen asleep –

all except one. Men well knew that the evil enemy
could not drag them down into the shadows
when it was against the Creator's wishes,
but Beowulf, watching grimly for his adversary Grendel,
awaited the ordeal with increasing anger.
Then, under night's shroud, Grendel walked down
from the moors; he shouldered God's anger.
The evil plunderer intended to ensnare
one of the race of men in the high hall.
He strode under the skies, until he stood
before the feasting-hall, in front of the gift-building
gleaming with gold. And this night was not the first
on which he had so honoured Hrothgar's home.
But never in his life did he find hall-wardens
more greatly to his detriment. Then the joyless warrior
journeyed to Heorot. The outer door, bolted
with iron bands, burst open at a touch from his hands:
with evil in his mind, and overriding anger,
Grendel swung open the hall's mouth itself. At once,
seething with fury, the fiend stepped onto
the tessellated floor; a horrible light,
like a lurid flame, flickered in his eyes.
He saw many men, a group of warriors,

a knot of kinsmen, sleeping in the hall.
His spirits leapt, his heart laughed;
the savage monster planned to sever,
before daybreak, the life of every warrior
from his body – he fully expected to eat
his fill at the feast. But after that night
fate decreed that he should no longer feed off
human flesh. Hygelac's kinsman,
the mighty man, watched the wicked ravager
to see how he would make his sudden attacks.
The monster was not disposed to delay;
but, for a start, he hungrily seized
a sleeping warrior, greedily wrenched him,
bit into his body, drank the blood
from his veins, devoured huge pieces;
until, in no time, he had swallowed the whole man,
even his feet and hands. Now Grendel stepped forward,
nearer and nearer, made to grasp the valiant Geat
stretched out on his bed – the fiend reached towards him
with his open hand; at once Beowulf perceived
his evil plan, sat up and stayed Grendel's outstretched
    arm.
Instantly that monster, hardened by crime,

realized that never had he met any man
in the regions of earth, in the whole world,
with so strong a grip. He was seized with terror.
But, for all that, he was unable to break away.
He was eager to escape to his lair, seek the company
of devils, but he was restrained as never before.
Then Hygelac's brave kinsman bore in mind
his boast: he rose from the bed and gripped
Grendel fiercely. The fiend tried to break free,
his fingers were bursting. Beowulf kept with him.
The evil giant was desperate to escape,
if indeed he could, and head for his lair
in the fens; he could feel his fingers cracking
in his adversary's grip; that was a bitter journey
that Grendel made to the ring-hall Heorot.
The great room boomed; all the proud warriors —
each and every Dane living in the stronghold —
were stricken with panic. The two hall-wardens
were enraged. The building rang with their blows.
It was a wonder the wine-hall withstood
two so fierce in battle, that the fair building
did not fall to earth; but it stood firm,
braced inside and out with hammered

iron bands. I have heard tell that there,
where they fought, many a mead-bench,
studded with gold, started from the floor.
Until that time, elders of the Scyldings
were of the opinion that no man could wreck
the great hall Heorot, adorned with horns,
nor by any means destroy it unless it were gutted
by greedy tongues of flame. Again and again
clang and clatter shattered the night's silence;
dread numbed the North-Danes, seized all
who heard the shrieking from the wall,
the enemy of God's grisly lay of terror,
his song of defeat, heard hell's captive
keening over his wound. Beowulf held him fast,
he who was the strongest of all men
ever to have seen the light of life on earth.
By no means did the defender of thanes
allow the murderous caller to escape with his life;
he reckoned that the rest of Grendel's days
were useless to anyone. Then, time and again,
Beowulf's band brandished their ancestral swords;
they longed to save the life, if they
so could, of their lord, the mighty leader.

When they did battle on Beowulf's behalf,
struck at the monster from every side,
eager for his end, those courageous warriors
were unaware that no war-sword,
not even the finest iron on earth,
could wound their evil enemy,
for he had woven a secret spell
against every kind of weapon, every battle blade.
Grendel's death, his departure from this world,
was destined to be wretched, his migrating spirit
was fated to travel far into the power of fiends.
Then he who for years had committed crimes
against mankind, murderous in mind,
and had warred with God, discovered
that the strength of his body could not save him,
that Hygelac's brave kinsman held his hand
in a vice-like grip; each was a mortal enemy
to the other. The horrible monster
suffered grievous pain; a gaping wound
opened on his shoulder; the sinews sprang apart,
the muscles were bursting. Glory in battle
was given to Beowulf; fatally wounded,
Grendel was obliged to make for the marshes,

head for his joyless lair. He was
well aware that his life's days were done,
come to an end. After that deadly encounter
the desire of every Dane was at last accomplished.

In this way did the wise and fearless man
who had travelled from far cleanse Hrothgar's hall,
release it from affliction. He rejoiced in his night's work,
his glorious achievement. The leader of the Geats
made good his boast to the East-Danes;
he had removed the cause of their distress,
put an end to the sorrow every Dane had shared,
the bitter grief that they had been constrained
to suffer. When Beowulf, brave in battle,
placed hand, arm and shoulder – Grendel's
entire grasp – under Heorot's spacious roof,
that was evidence enough of victory.

Then I have heard that next morning
many warriors gathered round the gift-hall;
leaders of men came from every region,
from remote parts, to look on the wonder,
the tracks of the monster. Grendel's death
seemed no grievous loss to any of the men
who set eyes on the spoor of the defeated one,

saw how he, weary in spirit, overcome in combat,
fated and put to flight, had made for the lake
of water-demons – leaving tracks of life-blood.

There the water boiled because of the blood;
the fearful swirling waves reared up,
mingled with hot blood, battle gore;
fated, he hid himself, then joyless
laid aside his life, his heathen spirit,
in the fen lair; hell received him there.

After this, the old retainers left the lake
and so did the company of young men too;
brave warriors rode back on their gleaming horses
from this joyful journey. Then Beowulf's exploit
was acclaimed; many a man asserted
time and again that there was no better
shield-bearer in the whole world, to north or south
between the two seas, under the sky's expanse,
no man more worthy of his own kingdom.
Yet they found no fault at all with their friendly lord,
gracious Hrothgar – he was a great king.

At times the brave warriors spurred their bays,
horses renowned for their speed and stamina,
and raced each other where the track was suitable.

And now and then one of Hrothgar's thanes
who brimmed with poetry, and remembered lays,
a man acquainted with ancient traditions
of every kind, composed a new song
in correct metre. Most skilfully that man
began to sing of Beowulf's feat,
to weave words together, and fluently
to tell a fitting tale.
                        He recounted all he knew
of Sigemund, the son of Wæls; many a strange story
about his exploits, his endurance, and his journeys
to earth's ends; many an episode
unknown or half-known to the sons of men, songs
of feud and treachery. Only Fitela knew of these things,
had heard them from Sigemund who liked to talk
of this and that, for he and his nephew
had been companions in countless battles —
they slew many monsters with their swords.
After his death, no little fame attached to Sigemund's
    name,
when the courageous man had killed the dragon,
guardian of the hoard. Under the grey rock
the son of the prince braved that dangerous deed

alone; Fitela was not with him;
for all that, as fate had it, he impaled
the wondrous serpent, pinned it to the rock face
with his patterned sword; the dragon was slain.
Through his own bravery, that warrior ensured
that he could enjoy the treasure hoard
at will; the son of Wæls loaded it all
onto a boat, stowed the shining treasure
into the ship; the serpent burned in its own flames.
Because of all his exploits, Sigemund,
guardian of strong men, was the best known
warrior in the world — so greatly had he prospered —
after Heremod's prowess, strength and daring
had been brought to an end, when, battling with giants,
he fell into the power of fiends, and was at once
done to death. He had long endured
surging sorrows, had become a source
of grief to his people, and to all his retainers.
And indeed, in those times now almost forgotten,
many wise men often mourned that great warrior,
for they had looked to him to remedy their miseries;
they thought that the prince's son would prosper
and attain his father's rank, would protect his people,

their heirlooms and their citadel, the heroes' kingdom,
land of the Scyldings. Beowulf, Hygelac's kinsman,
was much loved by all who knew him,
by his friends; but Heremod was stained by sin.
    Now and then the brave men raced their horses,
ate up the sandy tracks — and they were so absorbed
that the hours passed easily. Stout-hearted warriors
without number travelled to the high hall
to inspect that wonder; the king himself, too,
glorious Hrothgar, guardian of ring-hoards,
came from his quarters with a great company, escorted
his queen and her retinue of maidens into the mead-hall.
Hrothgar spoke — he approached Heorot,
stood on the steps, stared at the high roof
adorned with gold, and at Grendel's hand:
'Let us give thanks at once to God Almighty
for this sight. I have undergone many afflictions,
grievous outrages at Grendel's hands; but God,
Guardian of heaven, can work wonder upon wonder.
Until now, I had been resigned,
had no longer believed that my afflictions
would ever end: this finest of buildings
stood stained with battle blood,

a source of sorrow to my counsellors;
they all despaired of regaining this hall
for many years to come, of guarding it from foes,
from devils and demons. Yet now one warrior
alone, through the Almighty's power, has succeeded
where we failed for all our fine plans.
Indeed, if she is still alive,
that woman (whoever she was) who gave birth
to such a son, to be one of humankind,
may claim that the Creator was gracious to her
in her child-bearing. Now, Beowulf,
best of men, I will love you in my heart
like a son; keep to our new kinship
from this day on. You shall lack
no earthly riches I can offer you.
Most often I have honoured a man for less,
given treasure to a poorer warrior,
more sluggish in the fight. Through your deeds
you have ensured that your glorious name
will endure for ever. May the Almighty grant you
good fortune, as He has always done before!'
    Beowulf, the son of Ecgtheow, answered:
'We performed that dangerous deed

with good will; at peril we pitted ourselves
against the unknown. I wish so much
that you could have seen him for yourself,
that fiend in his trappings, in the throes of death.
I meant to throttle him on that bed of slaughter
as swiftly as possible, with savage grips,
to hear death rattle in his throat
because of my grasp, unless he should escape me.
But I could not detain him, the Lord
did not ordain it – I did not hold my deadly enemy
firm enough for that; the fiend jerked free
with immense power. Yet, so as to save
his life, he left behind his hand,
his arm and shoulder; but the wretched monster
has brought himself scant respite;
the evil marauder, tortured by his sins,
will not live the longer, but agony
embraces him in its deadly bonds,
squeezes life out of his lungs; and now this creature,
stained with crime, must await the day of judgement
and his just deserts from the glorious Creator.'
After this, the son of Ecglaf boasted less
about his prowess in battle – when all the warriors,

through Beowulf's might, had been enabled
to examine that hand, the fiend's fingers,
nailed up on the gables. Seen from in front,
each nail, each claw of that warlike,
heathen monster looked like steel –
a terrifying spike. Everyone said
that no weapon whatsoever, no proven sword
could possibly harm it, could damage
that battle-hardened, blood-stained hand.
   Then orders were quickly given for the inside of Heorot
to be decorated; many servants, both men and women,
bustled about that wine-hall, adorned that building
of retainers. Tapestries, worked in gold,
glittered on the walls, many a fine sight
for those who have eyes to see such things.
That beautiful building, braced within
by iron bands, was badly damaged;
the door's hinges were wrenched; when the monster,
damned by all his crimes, turned in flight,
despairing of his life, the hall roof only
remained untouched. Death is not easy
to escape, let him who will attempt it.
Man must go to the grave that awaits him –

fate has ordained this for all who have souls,
children of men, earth's inhabitants —
and his body, rigid on its clay bed,
will sleep there after the banquet.

                             Then it was time
for Healfdene's son to proceed to the hall,
the king himself was eager to attend the feast.
I have never heard of a greater band of kinsmen
gathered with such dignity around their ring-giver.
Then the glorious warriors sat on the benches,
rejoicing in the feast. Courteously
their kinsmen, Hrothgar and Hrothulf,
quaffed many a mead-cup, confident warriors
in the high hall. Heorot was packed
with feasters who were friends; the time was not yet come
when the Scyldings practised wrongful deeds.
Then Hrothgar gave Beowulf Healfdene's sword,
and a battle banner, woven with gold,
and a helmet and a corslet, as rewards for victory;
many men watched while the priceless, renowned sword
was presented to the hero. Beowulf emptied
the ale-cup in the hall; he had no cause
to be ashamed at those precious gifts.

There are few men, as far as I have heard,
who have given four such treasures, gleaming with gold,
to another on the mead-bench with equal generosity.
A jutting ridge, wound about with metal wires,
ran over the helmet's crown, protecting the skull,
so that well-ground swords, proven in battle,
could not injure the well-shielded warrior
when he advanced against his foes.
Then the guardian of thanes ordered
that eight horses with gold-plated bridles
be led into the courtyard; onto one was strapped
a saddle, inlaid with jewels, skilfully made.
That was the war-seat of the great king,
Healfdene's son, whenever he wanted
to join in the sword-play. That famous man
never lacked bravery at the front in battle,
when men about him were cut down like corn.
Then the king of the Danes, Ing's descendants,
presented the horses and weapons to Beowulf,
bade him use them well and enjoy them.
Thus the renowned prince, the retainers' gold-warden,
rewarded those fierce sallies in full measure,
with horses and treasure, so that no man

would ever find reason to reproach him fairly.
Furthermore, the guardian of warriors gave
a treasure, an heirloom at the mead-bench,
to each of those men who had crossed the sea
with Beowulf; and he ordered that gold
be paid for that warrior Grendel slew
so wickedly — as he would have slain many another,
had not foreseeing God and the warrior's courage
together forestalled him. The Creator ruled over
all humankind, even as He does today.
Wherefore a wise man will value forethought
and understanding. Whoever lives long
on earth, endures the unrest of these times,
will be involved in much good and much evil.
    Then Hrothgar, leader in battle, was entertained
with music — harp and voice in harmony.
The strings were plucked, many a song rehearsed,
when it was the turn of Hrothgar's poet
to please men at the mead-bench, perform
                                            in the hall.
He sang of Finn's troop, victims of surprise attack,
and of how that Danish hero, Hnæf of the Scyldings,
was destined to die among the Frisian slain.

Hildeburh, indeed, could hardly recommend
the honour of the Jutes; that innocent woman
lost her loved ones, son and brother,
in the shield-play; they fell, as fate ordained,
stricken by spears; and she was stricken with grief.
Not without cause did Hoc's daughter
mourn the shaft of fate, for in the light of morning
she saw that her kin lay slain under the sky,
the men who had been her endless pride
and joy. That encounter laid claim
to all but a few of Finn's thanes,
and he was unable to finish that fight
with Hnæf's retainer, with Hengest in the hall,
unable to dislodge the miserable survivors;
indeed, terms for a truce were agreed:
that Finn should give up to them another hall,
with its high seat, in its entirety,
which the Danes should own in common with the Jutes;
and that at the treasure-giving the son of Folcwalda
should honour the Danes day by day,
should distribute rings and gold-adorned gifts
to Hengest's band and his own people in equal measure.
Both sides pledged themselves to this peaceful

settlement. Finn swore Hengest solemn oaths
that he would respect the sad survivors
as his counsellors ordained, and that no man there
must violate the covenant with word or deed,
or complain about it, although they
would be serving the slayer of their lord
(as fate had forced those lordless men to do);
and he warned the Frisians that if, in provocation,
they should mention the murderous feud,
the sword's edge should settle things.
The funeral fire was prepared, glorious gold
was brought up from the hoard: the best of Scyldings,
that race of warriors, lay ready on the pyre.
Blood-stained corslets, and images of boars
(cast in iron and covered in gold)
were plentiful on that pyre, and likewise the bodies
of many retainers, ravaged by wounds;
renowned men fell in that slaughter.
Then Hildeburh asked that her own son
be committed to the flames at her brother's funeral,
that his body be consumed on Hnæf's pyre.
That grief-stricken woman keened over his corpse,
sang doleful dirges. The warriors' voices

soared towards heaven. And so did the smoke
from the great funeral fire that roared
before the barrow; heads sizzled,
wounds split open, blood burst out
from battle scars. The ravenous flames
swallowed those men whole, made no distinction
between Frisians and Danes; the finest men departed.
Then those warriors, their friends lost to them,
went to view their homes, revisit the stronghold
and survey the Frisian land. But Hengest
stayed with Finn, in utter dejection, all through
that blood-stained winter. And he dreamed
of his own country, but he was unable to steer
his ship homeward, for the storm-beaten sea
wrestled with the wind; winter sheathed the waves
in ice – until once again spring made its sign
(as still it does) among the houses of men:
clear days, warm weather, in accordance as always
with the law of the seasons. Then winter was over,
the face of the earth was fair; the exile
was anxious to leave that foreign people
and the Frisian land. And yet he brooded
more about vengeance than about a voyage,

and wondered whether he could bring about a clash
so as to repay the sons of the Jutes.
Thus Hengest did not shrink from the duty of vengeance
after Hunlafing had placed the flashing sword,
finest of all weapons, on his lap;
this sword's edges had scarred many Jutes.
And so it was that cruel death by the sword later
cut down the brave warrior Finn in his own hall,
after Guthlaf and Oslaf, arrived from a sea-journey,
had fiercely complained of that first attack,
condemned the Frisians on many scores:
the Scyldings' restless spirits could no longer
be restrained. Then the hall ran red with the blood
of the enemy – Finn himself was slain,
the king with his troop, and Hildeburh was taken.
The Scylding warriors carried that king's
heirlooms down to their ship,
all the jewels and necklaces they discovered
at Finn's hall. They sailed over the sea-paths,
brought that noble lady back to Denmark
and her own people.
                        Thus was the lay sung,
the song of the poet. The hall echoed with joy,

waves of noise broke out along the benches;
cup-bearers carried wine in glorious vessels.
Then Wealhtheow, wearing her golden collar, walked
to where Hrothgar and Hrothulf were sitting side by side,
uncle and nephew, still friends together, true to one
    another.
And the spokesman Unferth sat at the feet
of the Danish lord; all men admired
his spirit and audacity, although he had deceived
his own kinsmen in a feud. Then the lady of the Scyldings
spoke these words: 'Accept this cup, my loved lord,
treasure-giver; O gold-friend of men,
learn the meaning of joy again, and speak words
of gratitude to the Geats, for so one ought to do.
And be generous to them too, mindful of gifts
which you have now amassed from far and wide.
I am told you intend to adopt this warrior,
take him for your son. This resplendent ring-hall,
Heorot, has been cleansed; give many rewards
while you may, but leave this land and the Danish people
to your own descendants when the day comes
for you to die. I am convinced
that gracious Hrothulf will guard our children

justly, should he outlive you, lord of the Scyldings,
in this world; I believe he will repay our sons
most generously if he remembers all we did
for his benefit and enjoyment when he was a boy.'
Then Wealhtheow walked to the bench where her sons,
Hrethric and Hrothmund, sat with the sons of thanes,
fledgling warriors; where also that brave man,
Beowulf of the Geats, sat beside the brothers.
To him she carried the cup, and asked in gracious words
if he would care to drink; and to him she presented
twisted gold with courtly ceremonial —
two armlets, a corslet and many rings,
and the most handsome collar in the world.
I have never heard that any hero had a jewel
to equal that, not since Hama made off
for his fortress with the Brosings' necklace, that pendant
in its precious setting; he fled from the enmity
of underhand Eormenric, he chose long-lasting gain.
Hygelac the Geat, grandson of Swerting,
wore that necklace on his last raid
when he fought beneath his banner to defend his
    treasure,
his battle spoils; fate claimed him then,

when he, foolhardy, courted disaster,
a feud with the Frisians. On that occasion the famous
    prince
had carried the treasure, the priceless stones,
over the cup of the waves; he crumpled under his shield.
Then the king's body fell into the hands of Franks,
his coat of mail and the collar also;
after that battle, weaker warriors picked at
and plundered the slain; many a Geat lay dead guarding
that place of corpses.
                         Applause echoed in the hall.
Wealhtheow spoke these words before the company:
'May you, Beowulf, beloved youth, enjoy
with all good fortune this necklace and corslet,
treasures of the people; may you always prosper;
win renown through courage, and be kind in your
    counsel
to these boys; for that, I will reward you further.
You have ensured that men will always sing
your praises, even to the ends of the world,
as far as oceans still surround cliffs,
home of the winds. May you thrive, O prince,
all your life. I hope you will amass

a shining hoard of treasure. O happy Beowulf,
be gracious in your dealing with my sons.
Here, each warrior is true to the others,
gentle of mind, loyal to his lord;
the thanes are as one, the people all alert,
the warriors have drunk well. They will do as I ask.'

   Then Wealhtheow retired to her seat
beside her lord. That was the best of banquets,
men drank their fill of wine; they had not tasted
bitter destiny, the fate that had come and claimed
many of the heroes at the end of dark evenings,
when Hrothgar the warrior had withdrawn
to take his rest. Countless retainers
defended Heorot as they had often done before;
benches were pushed back; the floor was padded
with beds and pillows. But one of the feasters
lying on his bed was doomed, and soon to die.
They set their bright battle-shields
at their heads. Placed on the bench
above each retainer, his crested helmet,
his linked corslet and sturdy spear-shaft
were plainly to be seen. It was their habit,
both at home and in the field,

to be prepared for battle always,
for any occasion their lord might need
assistance; that was a loyal band of retainers.
   And so they slept. One man paid a heavy price
for his night's rest, as often happened
after Grendel first held the gold-hall
and worked his evil in it, until he met his doom,
death for his crimes. But afterwards it became clear,
and well known to the Scyldings, that some avenger
had survived the evil-doer, still lived after
that grievous, mortal combat.
                              Grendel's mother
was a monster of a woman; she mourned her fate —
she who had to live in the terrible lake,
the cold water streams, after Cain slew
his own brother, his father's son,
with a sword; he was outlawed after that;
a branded man, he abandoned human joys,
wandered in the wilderness. Many spirits, sent
by fate, issued from his seed; one of them, Grendel,
that hateful outcast, was surprised in the hall
by a vigilant warrior spoiling for a fight.
Grendel gripped and grabbed him there,

but the Geat remembered his vast strength,
that glorious gift given him of God,
and put his trust for support and assistance
in the grace of the Lord; thus he overcame
the envoy of hell, humbled his evil adversary.
So the joyless enemy of mankind journeyed
to the house of the dead. And then Grendel's mother,
mournful and ravenous, resolved to go
on a grievous journey to avenge her son's death.
     Thus she reached Heorot; Ring-Danes, snoring,
were sprawled about the floor. The thanes suffered
a serious reverse as soon as Grendel's mother
entered the hall. The terror she caused,
compared to her son, equalled the terror
an Amazon inspires as opposed to a man,
when the ornamented sword, forged on the anvil,
the razor-sharp blade stained with blood,
shears through the boar-crested helmets of the enemy.
Then swords were snatched from benches, blades
drawn from scabbards, many a broad shield
was held firmly in the hall; none could don helmet
or spacious corslet — that horror caught them by surprise.
The monster wanted to make off for the moors,

fly for her life, as soon as she was found out.
Firmly she grasped one of the thanes
and made for the fens as fast as she could.
That man whom she murdered even as he slept
was a brave shield-warrior, a well-known thane,
most beloved by Hrothgar of all his hall retainers
between the two seas. Beowulf was not there;
the noble Geat had been allotted another lodging
after the giving of treasure earlier that evening.
Heorot was in uproar; she seized her son's
blood-crusted hand; anguish once again
had returned to the hall. What kind of bargain
was that, in which both sides forfeited
the lives of friends?
                  Then the old king,
the grizzled warrior, was convulsed with grief
when he heard of the death of his dearest retainer.
    Immediately Beowulf, that man blessed with victory,
was called to the chamber of the king. At dawn
the noble warrior and his friends, his followers;
hurried to the room where the wise man was waiting,
waiting and wondering whether the Almighty
would ever allow an end to their adversity.

Then Beowulf, brave in battle, crossed
the floor with his band — the timbers thundered —
and greeted the wise king, overlord of Ing's
descendants; he asked if the night had passed off
peacefully, since his summons was so urgent.
    Hrothgar, guardian of the Scyldings, said:
'Do not speak of peace; grief once again
afflicts the Danish people. Yrmenlaf's
elder brother, Æschere, is dead,
my closest counsellor and my comrade,
my shoulder-companion when we shielded
our heads in the fight, when soldiers clashed on foot,
slashed at boar-crests. Æschere was all
that a noble man, a warrior should be.
The wandering, murderous monster slew him
in Heorot; and I do not know where that ghoul,
drooling at her feast of flesh and blood,
made off afterwards. She has avenged her son
whom you savaged yesterday with vice-like holds
because he had impoverished and killed my people
for many long years. He fell in mortal combat,
forfeit of his life; and now another mighty
evil ravager has come to avenge her kinsman;

and many a thane, mournful in his mind
for his treasure-giver, may feel she has avenged
that feud already, indeed more than amply;
now that hand lies still which once sustained you.

    I have heard my people say,
men of this country, counsellors in the hall,
that they have seen *two* such beings,
equally monstrous, rangers of the fell-country,
rulers of the moors; and these men assert
that so far as they can see one bears
a likeness to a woman; grotesque though he was,
the other who trod the paths of exile looked like a man,
though greater in height and build than a goliath;
he was christened *Grendel* by my people
many years ago; men do not know if he
had a father, a fiend once begotten
by mysterious spirits. These two live
in a little-known country, wolf-slopes, windswept
    headlands,
perilous paths across the boggy moors, where a mountain
    stream
plunges under the mist-covered cliffs,
rushes through a fissure. It is not far from here,

if measured in miles, that the lake stands
shadowed by trees stiff with hoar-frost.
A wood, firmly-rooted, frowns over the water.
There, night after night, a fearful wonder may be seen —
fire on the water; no man alive
is so wise as to know the nature of its depths.
Although the moor-stalker, the stag with strong horns,
when harried by hounds will make for the wood,
pursued from afar, he will succumb
to the hounds on the brink, rather than plunge in
and save his head. That is not a pleasant place.
When the wind arouses the wrath of the storm,
whipped waves rear up black from the lake,
reach for the skies, until the air becomes misty,
the heavens weep. Now, once again, help may be had
from you alone. As yet, you have not seen the haunt,
the perilous place where you may meet this most evil
    monster
face to face. Do you dare set eyes on it?
If you return unscathed, I will reward you
for your audacity, as I did before,
with ancient treasures and twisted gold.'
    Beowulf, the son of Ecgtheow, answered:

'Do not grieve, wise Hrothgar! Better each man
should avenge his friend than deeply mourn.
The days on earth for every one of us
are numbered; he who may should win renown
before his death; that is a warrior's
best memorial when he has departed from this world.
Come, O guardian of the kingdom, let us lose
no time but track down Grendel's kinswoman.
I promise you that wherever she turns —
to honeycomb caves, to mountain woods,
to the bottom of the lake she shall find no refuge.
Should your sorrows with patience
this day; this is what I expect of you.'
    Then the old king leaped up, poured out his gratitude
to God Almighty for the Geat's words.
Hrothgar's horse, his stallion with plaited mane,
was saddled and bridled; the wise ruler
set out in full array; his troop of shield-bearers
fell into step. They followed the tracks
along forest paths and over open hill-country
for mile after mile; the monster had made
for the dark moors directly, carrying the corpse
of the foremost thane of all those

who, with Hrothgar, had guarded the hall.
Then the man of noble lineage left Heorot far behind,
followed narrow tracks, string-thin paths
over steep, rocky slopes — remote parts
with beetling crags and many lakes
where water-demons lived. He went ahead
with a handful of scouts to explore the place;
all at once he came upon a dismal wood,
mountain trees standing on the edge
of a grey precipice; the lake lay beneath,
blood-stained and turbulent. The Danish retainers
were utterly appalled when they came upon
the severed head of their comrade Æschere
on the steep slope leading down to the lake;
all the thanes were deeply distressed.

    The water boiled with blood, with hot gore;
the warriors gaped at it. At times the horn sang
an eager battle-song. The brave men all sat down;
then they saw many serpents in the water,
strange sea-dragons swimming in the lake,
and also water-demons, lying on cliff-ledges,
monsters and serpents of the same kind
as often, in the morning, molest ships

on the sail-road. They plunged to the lake bottom,
bitter and resentful, rather than listen
to the song of the horn. The leader of the Geats
picked off one with his bow and arrow,
ended its life; its metal tip
stuck in its vitals; it swam more sluggishly
after that, as the life-blood ebbed from its body;
in no time this strange sea-dragon
bristled with barbed boar-spears, was subdued
and drawn up onto the cliff; men examined
that disgusting enemy.
              Beowulf donned
his coat of mail, did not fear for his own life.
His massive corslet, linked by hand
and skilfully adorned, was to essay the lake —
it knew how to guard the body, the bone-chamber,
so that his foe's grasp, in its malicious fury,
could not crush his chest, squeeze out his life;
and his head was guarded by the gleaming helmet
which was to explore the churning waters,
stir their very depths; gold decorated it,
and it was hung with chain-mail, as the weapon smith
had wrought it long before, wondrously shaped it

and beset it with boar-images, so that
afterwards no battle-blade could do it damage.
Not least amongst his mighty aids was Hrunting,
the long-hilted sword Unferth lent him in his need;
it was one of the finest of heirlooms; the iron blade
was engraved with deadly, twig-like patterning,
tempered with battle blood. It had not failed
any of those men who had held it in their hands,
risked themselves on hazardous exploits,
pitted themselves against foes. That was not
the first time it had to do a hard day's work.
Truly, when Ecglaf's son, himself so strong.
lent that weapon to his better as a swordsman,
he had forgotten all those taunts he flung
when tipsy with wine; he dared not chance
his own arm under the breakers, dared not
risk his life; at the lake he lost
his renown for bravery. It was not so with Beowulf
once he had armed himself for battle.
    The Geat, son of Ecgtheow, spoke:
'Great son of Healfdene, gracious ruler,
gold-friend of men, remember now —
for I am now ready to go —

what we agreed if I, fighting on your behalf,
should fail to return: that you would always
be like a father to me after I had gone.
Guard my followers, my dear friends,
if I die in battle; and, beloved Hrothgar,
send to Hygelac the treasures you gave me.
When the lord of the Geats, Hrethel's son,
sees those gifts of gold, he will know
that I found a noble giver of rings
and enjoyed his favour for as long as I lived.
And, O Hrothgar, let renowned Unferth
have the ancient treasure, the razor sharp
ornamented sword; and I will make my name
with Hrunting, or death will destroy me.'
    After these words the leader of the Geats
dived bravely from the bank, did not even
wait for an answer; the seething water
received the warrior. A full day elapsed
before he could discern the bottom of the lake.
    She who had guarded its length and breadth
for fifty years, vindictive, fiercely ravenous for blood,
soon realized that one of the race of men
was looking down into the monsters' lair.

Then she grasped him, clutched the Geat
in her ghastly claws; and yet she did not
so much as scratch his skin; his coat of mail
protected him; she could not penetrate
the linked metal rings with her loathsome fingers.
Then the sea-wolf dived to the bottom-most depths,
swept the prince to the place where she lived,
so that he, for all his courage, could not
wield a weapon; too many wondrous creatures
harassed him as he swam; many sea-serpents
with savage tusks tried to bore through his corslet,
the monsters molested him. Then the hero saw
that he had entered some loathsome hall
in which there was no water to impede him,
a vaulted chamber where the floodrush
could not touch him. A light caught his eye,
a lurid flame flickering brightly.

 Then the brave man saw the sea-monster,
fearsome, infernal; he whirled his blade,
swung his arm with all his strength,
and the ring-hilted sword sang a greedy war-song
on the monster's head. Then that guest realized
that his gleaming blade could not bite into her flesh,

break open her bone-chamber; its edge failed Beowulf
when he needed it; yet it had endured
many a combat, sheared often through the helmet,
split the corslet of a fated man; for the first time
that precious sword failed to live up to its name.

 Then, resolute, Hygelac's kinsman took his courage
in both hands, trusted in his own strength.
Angrily the warrior hurled Hrunting away,
the damascened sword with serpent patterns on its hilt;
tempered and steel-edged, it lay useless on the earth.
Beowulf trusted in his own strength,
the might of his hand. So must any man
who hopes to gain long-lasting fame
in battle; he must risk his life, regardless.
Then the prince of the Geats seized the shoulder
of Grendel's mother — he did not mourn their feud;
when they grappled, that brave man in his fury
flung his mortal foe to the ground.
Quickly she came back at him, locked him
in clinches and clutched at him fearsomely.
Then the greatest of warriors stumbled and fell.
She dropped on her hall-guest, drew her dagger,
broad and gleaming; she wanted to avenge her son,

her only offspring. The woven corslet
that covered his shoulders saved Beowulf's life,
denied access to both point and edge.
Then the leader of the Geats, Ecgtheow's son,
would have died far under the wide earth
had not his corslet, his mighty chain-mail,
guarded him, and had not holy God
granted him victory; the wise Lord,
Ruler of the Heavens, settled the issue
easily after the hero had scrambled to his feet.
    Then Beowulf saw among weapons an

                                    invincible sword
wrought by the giants, massive and double-edged,
the joy of many warriors; that sword was matchless,
well-tempered and adorned, forged in a finer age,
only it was so huge that no man but Beowulf
could hope to handle it in the quick of combat.
Ferocious in battle, the defender of the Scyldings
grasped the ringed hilt, swung the ornamented sword
despairing of his life — he struck such a savage blow
that the sharp blade slashed through her neck,
smashed the vertebrae; it severed her head
from the fated body; she fell at his feet.

The sword was bloodstained; Beowulf rejoiced.
    A light gleamed; the chamber was illumined
as if the sky's bright candle was shining
from heaven. Hygelac's thane inspected
the vaulted room, then walked round the walls,
fierce and resolute, holding the weapon firmly
by the hilt. The sword was not too large
for the hero's grasp, but he was eager to avenge
at once all Grendel's atrocities,
all the many visits the monster had inflicted
on the West-Danes – which began with the time
he slew Hrothgar's sleeping hearth-companions,
devoured fifteen of the Danish warriors
even as they slept, and carried off as many more,
a monstrous prize. But the resolute warrior
had already repaid him to such a degree
that he now saw Grendel lying on his death-bed,
his life's-blood drained because of the wound
he sustained in battle at Heorot. Then Grendel's corpse,
received a savage blow at the hero's hands,
his body burst open: Beowulf lopped off his head.
    At once the wise men, anxiously gazing at
the lake with Hrothgar, saw that the water

had begun to chop and churn, that the waves
were stained with blood. The grey-haired Scyldings
discussed that bold man's fate, agreed
there was no hope of seeing that brave thane again –
no chance that he would come, rejoicing in victory,
before their renowned king; it seemed certain
to all but a few that the sea-wolf had destroyed him.
    Then the ninth hour came. The noble Scyldings
left the headland; the gold-friend of men
returned to Heorot; the Geats, sick at heart,
sat down and stared at the lake.
Hopeless, they yet hoped to set eyes
on their dear lord.
                        Then the battle-sword
began to melt like a gory icicle
because of the monster's blood. Indeed,
it was a miracle to see it thaw entirely,
as does ice when the Father (He who ordains
all times and seasons) breaks the bonds of frost,
unwinds the flood fetters; He is the true Lord.
The leader of the Geats took none of the treasures
away from the chamber – though he saw many there –
except the monster's head and the gold-adorned

sword-hilt; the blade itself had melted,
the patterned sword had burnt, so hot was that blood,
so poisonous the monster who had died in the cave.
He who had survived the onslaught of his enemies
was soon on his way, swimming up through the water;
when the evil monster ended his days on earth,
left this transitory life, the troubled water
and all the lake's expanse was purged of its impurity.
      Then the fearless leader of the seafarers
swam to the shore, exulting in his plunder,
the heavy burdens he had brought with him.
The intrepid band of thanes hurried towards him,
giving thanks to God, rejoicing
to see their lord safe and sound of limb.
The brave man was quickly relieved of his helmet
and corslet.
                  The angry water under the clouds,
the lake stained with battle-blood, at last became calm.
      Then they left the lake with songs on their lips,
retraced their steps along the winding paths
and narrow tracks; it was no easy matter
for those courageous men, bold as kings,
to carry the head away from the cliff

overlooking the lake. With utmost difficulty
four of the thanes bore Grendel's head
to the gold-hall on a battle-pole;
thus the fourteen Geats, unbroken
in spirit and eager in battle, very soon
drew near to Heorot; with them, that bravest
of brave men crossed the plain towards the mead-hall.
Then the fearless leader of the thanes,
covered with glory, matchless in battle,
once more entered Heorot to greet Hrothgar.
Grendel's head was carried by the hair
onto the floor where the warriors were drinking,
a ghastly thing paraded before the heroes and the queen.
Men stared at that wondrous spectacle.

    Beowulf, the son of Ecgtheow, said:
'So, son of Healfdene, lord of the Scyldings,
we proudly lay before you plunder from the lake;
this head you look at proves our success.
I barely escaped with my life from that combat
under the water, the risk was enormous;
our encounter would have ended at once if God
had not guarded me. Mighty though it is,
Hrunting was no use at all in the battle;

but the Ruler of men – how often He guides
the friendless one – granted that I
should see a huge ancestral sword hanging,
shining, on the wall; I unsheathed it.
Then, at the time destiny decreed, I slew
the warden of the hall. And when the blood,
the boiling battle-blood burst from her body,
that sword burnt, the damascened blade
was destroyed. I deprived my enemies
of that hilt; I repaid them as they deserved
for their outrages, murderous slaughter of the Danes.
I promise, then, O prince of the Scyldings,
that you can sleep in Heorot without anxiety,
rest with your retainers, with all the thanes
among your people – experienced warriors
and striplings together – without further fear
of death's shadow skulking near the hall.'

    Then the golden hilt, age-old work of giants,
was given to Hrothgar, the grizzled warrior,
the warlike lord; wrought by master-smiths,
it passed into the hands of the Danish prince
once the demons died; for that embittered fiend,
enemy of God, guilty of murder

had abandoned this world — and so had his mother.
Thus the hilt was possessed by the best
of earthly kings between the two seas,
the best of those who bestowed gold on Norse men.
 Hrothgar spoke, first examining the hilt,
the ancient heirloom. On it was engraved
the origins of strife in time immemorial,
when the tide of rising water drowned
the race of giants; their end was horrible;
they were opposed to the Eternal Lord,
and their reward was the downpour and the flood.
Also, on the sword-guards of pure gold,
it was recorded in runic letters, as is the custom,
for whom that sword, finest of blades,
with twisted hilt and serpentine patterning
had first been made.
                         Then Healfdene's wise son
lifted his voice — everyone listened:
'This land's grizzled guardian, who promotes truth
and justice amongst his people, and forgets nothing
though the years pass, can say for certain that this man
is much favoured by fate! Beowulf my friend,
your name is echoed in every country

to earth's end. You wear your enormous might
with wisdom and with dignity. I shall keep
my promise made when last we spoke. You will
beyond doubt be the shield of the Geats
for days without number, and a source
of strength to warriors.
                            Heremod was hardly that
to Ecgwala's sons, the glorious Scyldings;
he grew to spread slaughter and destruction
rather than happiness amongst the Danish people.
In mad rage he murdered his table-companions,
his most loyal followers; it came about
that the great prince cut himself off
from all earthly pleasures, though God had
                                          endowed him
with strength and power above all other men,
and had sustained him. For all that, his heart
was filled with savage blood-lust. He never gave
gifts to the Danes, to gain glory. He lived joyless,
agony racked him; he was long an affliction
to his people. Be warned, Beowulf,
learn the nature of nobility. I who tell you
this story am many winters old.

                            It is a miracle
how the mighty Lord in his generosity
gives wisdom and land and high estate
to people on earth; all things are in His power.
At times he allows a noble man's mind to experience
happiness, grants he should rule over a pleasant,
prosperous country, a stronghold of men,
makes subject to him regions of earth,
a wide kingdom, until in his stupidity
there is no end to his ambition.
His life is unruffled – neither old age
nor illness afflict him, no unhappiness
gnaws at his heart, in his land no hatred
flares up in mortal feuds, but all the world
bends to his will. He suffers no setbacks
until the seed of arrogance is sown and grows
within him, while still the watchman slumbers;
how deeply the soul's guardian sleeps
when a man is enmeshed in matters of this world;
the evil archer stands close with his drawn bow,
his bristling quiver. Then the poisoned shaft
pierces his mind under his helmet
and he does not know how to resist

the devil's insidious, secret temptations.
What had long contented him now seems insufficient;
he becomes embittered, begins to hoard
his treasures, never parts with gold rings
in ceremonial splendour; he soon forgets
his destiny and disregards the honours
given him of God, the Ruler of Glory.
In time his transient body wizens and withers,
and dies as fate decrees; then another man
succeeds to his throne who gives treasures and heirlooms
with great generosity; *he* is not obsessed with suspicions.
Arm yourself, dear Beowulf, best of men,
against such diseased thinking; always swallow pride;
remember, renowned warrior, what is more worthwhile —
gain everlasting. Today and tomorrow
you will be in your prime; but soon you will die,
in battle or in bed; either fire or water,
the fearsome elements, will embrace you,
or you will succumb to the sword's flashing edge,
or the arrow's flight, or terrible old age;
then your eyes, once bright, will be clouded over;
all too soon, O warrior, death will destroy you.
    I have ruled the Ring-Danes under the skies

for fifty years, shielded them in war
from many tribes of men in this world,
from swords and from ash-spears, and the time had come
when I thought I had no enemies left on earth.
All was changed utterly, gladness
became grief, after Grendel,
my deadly adversary, invaded Heorot.
His visitations caused me continual pain.
Thus I thank the Creator, the Eternal Lord,
that after our afflictions I have lived to see,
to see with my own eyes this blood-stained head.
Now, Beowulf, brave in battle,
go to your seat and enjoy the feast;
tomorrow we shall share many treasures.'
     The Geat, full of joy, straightway went
to find his seat as Hrothgar had suggested.
Then, once again, as so often before,
a great feast was prepared for the brave warriors
sitting in the hall.
                    The shadows of night
settled over the retainers. The company arose;
the grey-haired man, the old Scylding,
wanted to retire. And the Geat, the shield-warrior,

was utterly exhausted, his bones ached for sleep.
At once the chamberlain — he who courteously
saw to all such needs as a thane,
a travelling warrior, had in those days —
showed him, so limb-weary, to his lodging.
     Then Beowulf rested; the building soared,
spacious and adorned with gold; the guest
slept within until the black raven gaily
proclaimed sunrise. Bright light
chased away the shadows of night.
                         Then the warriors
hastened, the thanes were eager to return
to their own people; the brave seafarer
longed to see his ship, so far from that place.
Then the bold Geat ordered that Hrunting,
that sword beyond price, be brought before Unferth;
he begged him to take it back and thanked him
for the loan of it; he spoke of it as an ally
in battle, and assured Unferth he did not
underrate it: what a brave man he was!
After this the warriors, wearing their chain-mail,
were eager to be off; their leader,
so dear to the Danes, walked to the daïs

where Hrothgar was sitting, and greeted him.
    Beowulf, the son of Ecgtheow, spoke:
'Now we seafarers, who have sailed here from far,
beg to tell you we are eager
to return to Hygelac. We have been happy here,
hospitably entertained; you have treated us kindly.
If I can in any way win more of your affection,
O ruler of men, than I have done already,
I will come at once, eager for combat.
If news reaches me over the seas
that you are threatened by those around you
(just as before enemies endangered you)
I will bring thousands of thanes,
all heroes, to help you. I know that Hygelac,
lord of the Geats, guardian of his people,
will advance me in word and deed
although he is young, so that I can back
these promises with spear shafts, and serve you
with all my strength where you need men.
Should Hrethric, Hrothgar's son, wish
to visit the court of the Geatish king,
he will be warmly welcomed. Strong men
should seek fame in far-off lands.'

Hrothgar replied: 'The wise Lord put these words
into your mind; I have never heard a warrior
speak more sagely while still so young.
You are very strong and very shrewd,
you speak with discerning. If your leader,
Hrethel's son, guardian of the people,
were to lose his life by illness or by iron,
by spear or grim swordplay, and if you survived him,
it seems to me that the Geats could not choose
a better man for king, should you wish to rule
the land of your kinsmen. Beloved Beowulf,
the longer I know you, the greater my regard for you.
Because of your exploit, your act of friendship,
there will be an end to the gross outrages,
the old enmity between Geats and Danes;
they will learn to live in peace.
For as long as I rule this spacious land,
heirlooms will be exchanged; many men
will greet their friends with gifts, send them
over the seas where gannets swoop and rise;
the ring-prowed ship will take tokens of esteem,
treasures across the water. I know the Geats
are honourable to friend and foe alike,

always faithful to their ancient code.'
    Then Healfdene's son, guardian of thanes,
gave him twelve treasures in the hall,
told him to go safely with those gifts
to his own dear kinsmen, and to come back soon.
That king, descendant of kings,
leader of the Scyldings, kissed and embraced
the best of thanes; tears streamed down
the old man's face. The more that warrior thought,
wise and old, the more it seemed
improbable that they would meet again,
brave men in council. He so loved Beowulf
that he could not conceal his sense of loss;
but in his heart and in his head,
in his very blood, a deep love burned
for that dear man.
                    Then Beowulf the warrior,
proudly adorned with gold, crossed the plain,
exulting in his treasure. The ship
rode at anchor, waiting for its owner.
Then, as they walked, they often praised
Hrothgar's generosity. He was an altogether
faultless king, until old age deprived him

of his strength, as it does most men.

Then that troop of brave young retainers
came to the water's edge; they wore ring-mail,
woven corslets. And the same watchman
who had seen them arrive saw them now returning.
He did not insult them, ask for explanations,
but galloped from the cliff-top to greet the guests;
he said that those warriors in gleaming armour,
so eager to embark, would be welcomed home.
Then the spacious ship, with its curved prow,
standing ready on the shore, was laden with armour,
with horses and treasure. The mast towered
over Hrothgar's precious heirlooms.

Beowulf gave a sword bound round with gold
to the ship's watchman — a man who thereafter
was honoured on the mead-bench that much the more
on account of this heirloom.

The ship surged forward,
butted the waves in deep waters;
it drew away from the shores of the Scyldings.
Then a sail, a great sea-garment, was fastened
with guys to the mast; the timbers groaned;
the boat was not blown off its course

by the stiff sea-breezes. The ship swept
over the waves; foaming at the bows,
the boat with its well-wrought prow sped
over the waters, until at last the Geats
set eyes on the cliffs of their own country,
the familiar headlands; the vessel pressed forward,
pursued by the wind — it ran up onto dry land.

    The harbour guardian hurried down to the shore;
for many days he had scanned the horizon,
anxious to see those dear warriors once more.
He tethered the spacious sea-steed with ropes
(it rode on its painter restlessly)
so that the rolling waves could not wrench it away.
Then Beowulf commanded that the peerless treasures,
the jewels and plated gold, be carried up from the shore.
He had not to go far to find the treasure-giver,
Hygelac son of Hrethel, for his house and the hall
for his companions stood quite close to the sea-wall.
That high hall was a handsome building;
it became the valiant king.

                Hygd, his queen,
Hæreth's daughter, was very young; but she
was discerning, and versed in courtly customs,

though she had lived a short time only
in that citadel; and she was not too thrifty,
not ungenerous with gifts of precious treasures
to the Geatish thanes.

                Queen Thryth was proud
and perverse, pernicious to her people.
No hero but her husband, however bold,
dared by day so much as turn his head
in her direction — that was far too dangerous;
but, if he did, he could bargain on being cruelly
bound with hand-plaited ropes; soon
after his seizure, the blade was brought into play,
the damascened sword to settle the issue,
to inflict death. It is not right for a queen,
compelling though her beauty, to behave like this,
for a peace-weaver to deprive a dear man of his life
because she fancies she has been insulted.
But Offa, Hemming's kinsman, put an end to that.
Ale-drinking men in the hall have said
that she was no longer perfidious to her people,
and committed no crimes, once she had been given,
adorned with gold, to that young warrior
of noble descent — once she had sailed,

at her father's command, to Offa's court
beyond the pale gold sea. After that,
reformed, she turned her life to good account;
renowned for virtue, she reigned with vision;
and she loved the lord of warriors in the high way
of love — he who was, as I have heard,
the best of all men, the mighty human race,
between the two seas. Offa the brave
was widely esteemed both for his gifts
and his skill in battle; he ruled his land
wisely. He fathered Eomer, guardian
of thanes, who was Hemming's kinsman,
grandson of Garmund, a goliath in battle.

    Then Beowulf and his warrior band walked
across the sand, tramped over
the wide foreshore; the world's candle shone,
the sun hastening from the south. The men hurried too
when they were told that the guardian of thanes,
Ongentheow's slayer, the excellent young king,
held court in the hall, distributing rings.
Hygelac was informed at once of Beowulf's arrival —
that the shield of warriors, his comrade in battle,
had come back alive to the fortified enclosure,

was heading for the hall unscathed after combat.
Space on the benches for Beowulf and his band
was hastily arranged, as Hygelac ordered.

    The guardian of thanes formally greeted
that loyal man; then they sat down —
the unfated hero opposite the king,
kinsman facing kinsman. Hœreth's daughter
carried mead-cups round the hall,
spoke kindly to the warriors, handed the stoups
of wine to the thanes. Hygelac began
to ask his companion courteous questions
in the high hall; he was anxious to hear
all that had happened to the seafaring Geats:
'Beloved Beowulf, tell me what became of you
after the day you so hurriedly decided
to do battle far from here over the salt waters,
to fight at Heorot. And were you able
to assuage the grief, the well-known sorrow
of glorious Hrothgar? Your undertaking
deeply troubled me; I despaired, dear Beowulf,
of your return. I pleaded with you
not on any account to provoke that monster,
but to let the South-Danes settle their feud

with Grendel themselves. God be praised
that I am permitted to see you safe and home.'
    Then Beowulf, the son of Ecgtheow, said:
'Half the world, lord Hygelac, has heard
of my encounter, my great combat
hand to hand with Grendel in that hall
where he had harrowed and long humiliated
the glorious Scyldings. I avenged it all;
none of Grendel's brood, however long
the last of that hateful race survives,
steeped in crime, has any cause to boast about
that dawn combat.
             First of all,
I went to the ring-hall to greet Hrothgar;
once Healfdene's great son knew of my intentions,
he assigned me a seat beside his own sons.
Then there was revelry; never in my life,
under heaven's vault, have I seen men
happier in the mead-hall. From time to time
the famous queen, the peace-weaver, walked across the
    floor,
exhorting the young warriors; often she gave
some man a twisted ring before returning to her seat.

At times Hrothgar's daughter, whom I heard
men call Freawaru, carried the ale-horn
right round the hall in front of that brave company,
offered that vessel adorned with precious metals
to the thirsty warriors.
                    Young, and decorated
with gold ornaments, she is promised to Froda's noble son,
Ingeld of the Heathobards; that match was arranged
by the lord of the Scyldings, guardian of the kingdom;
he believes that it is an excellent plan
to use her as a peace-weaver to bury old antagonisms,
mortal feuds. But the deadly spear rarely sleeps
for long after a prince lies dead in the dust,
however exceptional the bride may be!
    For Ingeld, leader of the Heathobards, and all
his retainers will later be displeased when he
and Freawaru walk on the floor — man and wife —
and when the Danish warriors are being entertained.
For the guests will gleam with Heathobard heirlooms,
iron-hard, adorned with rings,
precious possessions that had belonged
to their hosts' fathers for as long as they
could wield their weapons, until in the shield-play

they and their dear friends forfeited their lives.
Then, while men are drinking, an old
warrior will speak; a sword he has seen,
marvellously adorned, stirs his memory
of how Heathobards were slain by spears;
he seethes with fury; sad in heart,
he begins to taunt a young Heathobard,
incites him to action with these words:
    'Do you not recognize that sword, my friend,
the sword your father, fully armed, bore into battle
that last time, when he was slain by Danes,
killed by brave Scyldings who carried the field
when Withergyld fell and many warriors beside him?
See how the son of one of those
who slew him struts about the hall;
he sports the sword; he crows about that slaughter,
and carries that heirloom which is yours by right!'
In this way, with acid words, he will endlessly
provoke him and rake up the past,
until the time will come when a Danish warrior,
Freawaru's thane, sleeps blood-stained,
slashed by the sword, punished by death
for the deeds of his father; and the Heathobard

will escape, well-acquainted with the country.
Then both sides will break the solemn oath
sworn by their leaders; and Ingeld will come
to hate the Scyldings, and his love for his wife
will no longer be the same after such anguish and grief.
Thus I have little faith in friendship with Heathobards;
they will fail to keep their side of the promise,
friendship with the Danes.
                                I have digressed;
Grendel is my subject. Now you must hear,
O treasure-giver, what the outcome was
of that hand-to-hand encounter. When the jewel of
    heaven
had journeyed over the earth, the angry one,
the terrible night-prowler paid us a visit—
unscathed warriors watching over Heorot.
A fight awaited Hondscio, a horrible end
for that fated man; he was the first to fall;
Grendel tore that famous young retainer to bits
between his teeth, and swallowed the whole body
of that dear man, that girded warrior.
And even then that murderer, mindful of evil,
his mouth caked with blood, was not content

to leave the gold-hall empty-handed
but, famed for his strength, he tackled me,
gripped me with his outstretched hand.
A huge unearthly glove swung at his side,
firmly secured with subtle straps;
it had been made with great ingenuity,
with devils' craft and dragons' skins.
Innocent as I was, the demon monster
meant to shove me in it, and many another
innocent besides; that was beyond him
after I leapt up, filled with fury.
It would take too long to tell you how I repaid
that enemy of men for all his outrages;
but there, my prince, I ennobled your people
with my deeds. Grendel escaped,
and lived a little longer; but he left
behind at Heorot his right hand; and in utter
wretchedness, sank to the bottom of the lake.
  The sun rose; we sat down together
to feast, then the leader of the Scyldings
paid a good price for the bloody battle,
gave me many a gold-plated treasure.
There was talk and song; the grey-haired Scylding

opened his immense hoard of memories;
now and then a happy warrior touched
the wooden harp, reciting some story,
mournful and true; at times the generous king
recalled in proper detail some strange incident;
and as the shadows lengthened, an aged thane,
cramped and rheumatic, raised his voice
time and again, lamenting his lost youth,
his prowess in battle; worn with winters,
his heart quickened to the call of the past.

    In these ways we relaxed agreeably
throughout the long day until darkness closed in,
another night for men. Then, in her grief,
bent on vengeance, Grendel's mother
hastened to the hall where death had lain
in wait for her son – the battle-hatred
of the Geats. The horrible harridan avenged
her offspring, slew a warrior brazenly.
Æschere, the wise old counsellor, lost
his life. And when morning came,
the Danes were unable to cremate him,
to place the body of that dear man
on the funeral pyre; for Grendel's mother

had carried it off in her gruesome grasp,
taken it under the mountain lake.
Of all the grievous sorrows Hrothgar
long sustained, none was more terrible.
Then the king in his anger called upon your name
and entreated me to risk my life,
to accomplish deeds of utmost daring
in the tumult of waves; he promised me rewards.
And so, as men now know all over the earth,
I found the grim guardian of the lake-bottom.
For a while we grappled; the water boiled
with blood; then in that battle-hall,
I lopped off Grendel's mother's head
with the mighty sword. I barely escaped
with my life; but I was not fated.

    And afterwards the guardian of thanes,
Healfdene's son, gave me many treasures.
Thus the king observed excellent tradition:
in no wise did I feel unrewarded
for all my efforts, but Healfdene's son
offered me gifts of my own choosing;
gifts, O noble king, I wish now
to give to you in friendship. I still depend

entirely on your favours; I have few
close kinsmen but you, O Hygelac!'
    Then Beowulf caused to be brought in
a standard bearing the image of a boar,
together with a helmet towering in battle,
a grey corslet, and a noble sword; he said:
'Hrothgar, the wise king, gave me
these trappings and purposely asked me
to tell you their history: he said that Heorogar,
lord of the Scyldings, long owned them.
Yet he has not endowed his own brave son,
Heoroweard, with this armour, much as
he loves him. Make good use of everything!'
    I heard that four bays, apple-brown,
were brought into the hall after the armour —
swift as the wind, identical. Beowulf gave them
as he gave the treasures. So should a kinsman do,
and never weave nets with underhand subtlety
to ensnare others, never have designs
on a close comrade's life. His nephew,
brave in battle, was loyal to Hygelac;
each man was mindful of the other's pleasure.
    I heard that he gave Hygd the collar,

the wondrous ornament with which Wealhtheow,
daughter of the prince, had presented him,
and gave her three horses also, graceful creatures
with brightly-coloured saddles; Hygd
wore that collar, her breast was adorned.

   Thus Ecgtheow's son, feared in combat,
confirmed his courage with noble deeds;
he lived a life of honour, he never slew
companions at the feast, savagery was
alien to him, but he, so brave in battle,
made the best use of those ample talents
with which God endowed him.
                                        He had been despised
for a long while, for the Geats saw no spark
of bravery in him, nor did their king deem him
worthy of much attention on the mead-bench;
people thought that he was a sluggard,
a feeble princeling. How fate changed,
changed completely for that glorious man!

   Then the guardian of thanes, the famous king,
ordered that Hrethel's gold-adorned heirloom
be brought in; no sword was so treasured
in all Geatland; he laid it in Beowulf's lap,

and gave him seven thousand hides of land,
a hall and princely throne. Both men
had inherited land and possessions
in that country; but the more spacious kingdom
had fallen to Hygelac, who was of higher rank.

In later days, after much turmoil,
things happened in this way: when Hygelac lay dead
and murderous battle-blades had beaten down
the shield of his son Heardred,
and when the warlike Swedes, savage warriors,
had hunted him down amongst his glorious people,
attacked Hereric's nephew with hatred,
the great kingdom of the Geats passed
into Beowulf's hands. He had ruled it well
for fifty winters — he was a wise king,
a grizzled guardian of the land — when, on dark nights,
a dragon began to terrify the Geats:
he lived on a cliff, kept watch over a hoard
in a high stone barrow; below, there was
a secret path; a man strayed

into this barrow by chance, seized
some of the pagan treasures, stole drinking vessels.
At first the sleeping dragon was deceived
by the thief's skill, but afterwards he avenged
this theft of gleaming gold; people far and wide,
bands of retainers, became aware of his wrath.

That man did not intrude upon the hoard
deliberately, he who robbed the dragon;
but it was some slave, a wanderer in distress
escaping from men's anger who entered there,
seeking refuge. He stood guilty of some sin.
As soon as he peered in, the outsider
stiffened with horror. Unhappy as he was,
he stole the vessel, the precious cup.
There were countless heirlooms in that earth-cave,
the enormous legacy of a noble people,
ancient treasures which some man or other
had cautiously concealed there many years
before. Death laid claim to all that people
in days long past, and then that retainer
who outlived the rest, a gold-guardian
mourning his friends, expected the same fate —
thought he would enjoy those assembled heirlooms

a little while only. A newly-built barrow
stood ready on a headland which overlooked
the sea, protected by the hazards of access.
To this barrow the protector of rings brought the
  heirlooms,
the plated gold, all that part of the precious treasure
worthy of hoarding; then he spoke a few words:
'Hold now, O earth, since heroes could not,
these treasures owned by nobles! Indeed, strong men
first quarried them from you. Death in battle,
ghastly carnage, has claimed all my people —
men who once made merry in the hall
have laid down their lives; I have no one
to carry the sword, to polish the plated vessel,
this precious drinking-cup; all the retainers
have hurried elsewhere. The iron helmet
adorned with gold shall lose its ornaments;
men who should polish battle-masks are sleeping;
the coat of mail, too, that once withstood
the bite of swords in battle, after shields were shattered,
decays like the warriors; the linked mail may no longer
range far and wide with the warrior,
stand side by side with heroes. Gone is the pleasure

of plucking the harp, no fierce hawk
swoops about the hall, nor does the swift stallion
strike sparks in the courtyard. Cruel death
has claimed hundreds of this human race.'

Thus the last survivor mourned time passing,
and roamed about by day and night,
sad and aimless, until death's lightning
struck at his heart.

The aged dragon of darkness
discovered that glorious hoard unguarded,
he who sought out barrows, smooth-scaled
and evil, and flew by night, breathing
fire; the Geats feared him greatly.
He was destined to find the hoard
in that cave and, old in winters, guard
the heathen gold; much good it did him!

Thus the huge serpent who harassed men
guarded that great stronghold under the earth
for three hundred winters, until
a man enraged him; the wanderer carried
the inlaid vessel to his lord, and begged him
for a bond of peace. Then the hoard was raided
and plundered, and that unhappy man

was granted his prayer. His lord examined
the ancient work of smiths for the first time.
    There was conflict once more after the dragon
awoke; intrepid, he slid swiftly
along by the rock, and found the footprints
of the intruder; that man had skilfully
picked his way right past the dragon's head.
Thus he who is undoomed will easily survive
anguish and exile provided he enjoys
the grace of God. The warden of the hoard
prowled up and down, anxious to find
the man who had pillaged it while he slept.
Breathing fire and filled with fury,
he circled the outside of the earth mound
again and again; but there was no one
in that barren place; yet he exulted at the thought
of battle, bloody conflict; at times he wheeled back
into the barrow, hunting for the priceless heirloom.
He realized at once that one of the race of men
had discovered the gold, the glorious treasure.
Restlessly the dragon waited for darkness;
the guardian of the hoard was bursting with rage,
he meant to avenge the vessel's theft

with fire.
　　　　Then daylight failed
as the dragon desired; he could no longer
confine himself to the cave but flew in a ball
of flame, burning for vengeance. The Geats
were filled with dread as he began his flight;
it swiftly ended in disaster for their lord.
　　Then the dragon began to breathe forth fire,
to burn fine buildings; flame tongues flickered,
terrifying men; the loathsome winged creature
meant to leave the whole place lifeless.
Everywhere the violence of the dragon, the venom
of that hostile one, was clearly to be seen —
how he had wrought havoc, hated and humiliated
the Geatish people. Then, before dawn he rushed back
to his hidden lair and the treasure hoard.
He had girdled the Geats with fire,
with ravening flames; he relied on his own strength,
and on the barrow and the cliff; his trust played
　　　　　　　　　　　　　　　　him false.
Then news of that terror was quickly brought
to Beowulf, that flames eveloped
his own hall, best of buildings,

and the gift-throne of the Geats. That good man
was choked with intolerable grief.
Wise that he was, he imagined
he must have angered God, the Lord Eternal,
by ignoring some ancient law; he was seldom
dispirited, but now his heart was like lead.
　　The fire dragon had destroyed the fortified hall,
the people's stronghold, and laid waste with flames
the land by the sea. The warlike king,
prince of the Geats, planned to avenge this.
The protector of warriors, leader of men,
instructed the smith to forge a curious shield
made entirely of iron; he well knew
that a linden shield would not last long
against the flames. The eminent prince
was doomed to reach the end of his days on earth,
his life in this world. So too was the dragon,
though he had guarded the hoard for generations.
　　Then the giver of gold disdained
to track the dragon with a troop
of warlike men; he did not shrink
from single combat, nor did he set much store
by the fearless dragon's power, for had he not before

experienced danger, again and again
survived the storm of battle, beginning with that time
when, blessed with success, he cleansed
Hrothgar's hall, and crushed in battle
the monster and his vile mother?

                       That grim combat
in which Hygelac was slain — Hrethel's son,
leader of the Geats, dear lord of his people,
struck down by swords in the bloodbath
in Frisia — was far from the least
of his encounters. Beowulf escaped
because of his skill and stamina at swimming;
he waded into the water, bearing no fewer
than thirty corslets, a deadweight on his arms.
But the Frankish warriors who shouldered
their shields against him had no cause to boast
about that combat; a handful only
eluded that hero and returned home.
Then the son of Ecgtheow, saddened and alone,
rode with the white horses to his own people.
Hygd offered him heirlooms there, and even
the kingdom, the ancestral throne itself; for she feared
that her son would be unable to defend it

from foreign invaders now that Hygelac was gone.
But the Geats, for all their anguish, failed
to prevail upon the prince – he declined
absolutely to become Heardred's lord,
or to taste the pleasures of royal power.
But he stood at his right hand,
ready with advice, always friendly,
and respectful, until the boy came of age
and could rule the Geats himself.

       Two exiles,
Ohthere's sons, sailed to Heardred's court;
they had rebelled against the ruler of the Swedes,
a renowned man, the best of sea-kings,
gold-givers in Sweden. By receiving them,
Heardred rationed the days of his life;
in return for his hospitality, Hygelac's son
was mortally wounded, slashed by swords.
Once Heardred lay lifeless in the dust,
Onela, son of Ongentheow, sailed home again;
he allowed Beowulf to inherit the throne
and rule the Geats; he was a noble king!
But Beowulf did not fail with help
after the death of the prince, although years passed;

he befriended unhappy Eadgils, Ohthere's son,
and supplied him with weapons and warriors
beyond the wide seas. Eadgils afterwards
avenged Eanmund, he ravaged and savaged
the Swedes, and killed the king, Onela himself.
   Thus the son of Ecgtheow had survived
these feuds, these fearful battles, these acts
of single combat, up to that day
when he was destined to fight against the dragon.
Then in fury the leader of the Geats set out
with eleven to search for the winged serpent.
By then Beowulf knew the cause of the feud,
bane of men; the famous cup
had come to him through the hands of its finder.
The unfortunate slave who first brought about
such strife made the thirteenth man
in that company – cowed and disconsolate,
he had to be their guide. Much against his will,
he conducted them to the entrance of the cave,
an earth-hall full of filigree work
and fine adornments close by the sea,
the fretting waters. The vile guardian,
the serpent who had long lived under the earth,

watched over the gold, alert; he who hoped
to gain it bargained with his own life.
   Then the brave king sat on the headland,
the gold-friend of the Geats wished success
to his retainers. His mind was most mournful,
angry, eager for slaughter; fate hovered
over him, so soon to fall on that old man,
to seek out his hidden spirit, to split
life and body; flesh was to confine
the soul of the king only a little longer.
Beowulf, the son of Ecgtheow, spoke:
'Often and often in my youth I plunged
into the battle maelstrom; how well I remember it.
I was seven winters old when the treasure guardian,
ruler of men, received me from my father.
King Hrethel took me into his ward, reared me,
fed me, gave me gold, mindful of our kinship;
for as long as he lived, he loved me no less
than his own three sons, warriors with me
in the citadel, Herebeald, Hæthcyn, and my dear
   Hygelac.
A death-bed for the firstborn was unrolled
most undeservedly by the action of his kinsman —

Hæthcyn drew his horn-tipped bow
and killed his lord-to-be; he missed his mark,
his arrow was stained with his brother's blood.
That deed was a dark sin, sickening
to think of, not to be settled by payment of *wergild*;
yet Herebeald's death could not be requited.

  Thus the old king, Hrethel, is agonized
to see his son, so young, swing
from the gallows. He sings a dirge, a song
dark with sorrow, while his son hangs,
raven's carrion, and he cannot help him
in any way, wise and old as he is.
He wakes each dawn to the ache
of his son's death; he has no desire
for a second son, to be his heir
in the stronghold, now that his firstborn
has finished his days and deeds on earth.
Grieving, he wanders through his son's dwelling,
sees the wine-hall now deserted, joyless,
home of the winds; the riders, the warriors,
sleep in their graves. No longer is the harp
plucked, no longer is there happiness in that place.
Then Hrethel takes to his bed, and intones

dirges for his dead son, Herebeald;
his house and his lands seem empty now,
and far too large. Thus the lord of the Geats
endured in his heart the ebb and flow
of sorrow for his firstborn; but he could not
avenge that feud on the slayer – his own son;
although Hrethel had no love for Hæthcyn,
he could no more readily requite death
with death. Such was his sorrow that he lost
all joy in life, chose the light of God;
he bequeathed to his sons, as a wealthy man does,
his citadel and land, when he left this life.

  Then there was strife, savage conflict
between Swedes and Geats; after Hrethel's death
the feud we shared, the fierce hatred
flared up across the wide water.
The sons of Ongentheow, Onela and Ohthere,
were brave and battle-hungry; they had no wish
for peace over the sea but several times,
and wantonly, butchered the people of the Geats
on the slopes of Slaughter Hill. As is well known,
my kinsmen requited that hatred, those crimes;
but one of them paid with his own life –

a bitter bargain; that fight was fatal
to Hæthcyn, ruler of the Geats.
Then I heard that in the morning
one kinsman avenged another, repaid
Hæthcyn's slayer with the battle-blade,
when Ongentheow attacked the Geat Eofor;
the helmet split, the old Swede fell,
pale in death; Eofor remembered
that feud well enough, his hand and sword
spared nothing in their death-swing.

    I repaid Hygelac for his gifts of heirlooms
with my gleaming blade, repaid him in battle,
as was granted to me; he gave me land
and property, a happy home. He had
no need to hunt out and hire mercenaries —
inferior warriors from the Gepidae,
from the Spear-Danes or from tribes in Sweden;
but I was always at the head of his host,
alone in the van; and I shall still fight
for as long as I live and this sword lasts,
that has often served me early and late
since I became the daring slayer
of Dæghrefn, champion of the Franks.

He was unable to bring adornments,
breast-decorations to the Frisian king,
but fell in the fight bearing the standard,
a brave warrior; it was my battle-grip,
not the sharp blade, that shattered his bones,
silenced his heartbeat. Now the shining edge,
hand and tempered sword, shall engage in battle
for the treasure hoard. I fought many battles
when I was young; yet I will fight again,
the old guardian of my people, and achieve
a mighty exploit if the evil dragon dares
confront me, dares come out of the earth-cave!'

    Then he addressed each of the warriors,
the brave heroes, his dear companions,
a last time: 'I would not wield a sword
against the dragon if I could grasp this hideous being
with my hands (and thus make good my boast),
as once I grasped the monster Grendel;
but I anticipate blistering battle-fire,
venomous breath; therefore I have with me
my shield and corslet. I will not give an inch
to the guardian of the mound, but at that barrow
it will befall us both as fate ordains,

every man's master. My spirit is bold,
I will not boast further against the fierce flier.
Watch from the barrow, warriors in armour,
guarded by corslets, which of us will better
weather his wounds after the combat.
This is not your undertaking, nor is it
possible for any man but me alone
to pit his strength against the gruesome one,
and perform great deeds. I will gain the gold
by daring, or else battle, dread destroyer
of life, will lay claim to your lord.'

    Then the bold warrior, stern-faced beneath his helmet,
stood up with his shield; sure of his own strength,
he walked in his corslet towards the cliff;
the way of the coward is not thus!
Then that man endowed with noble qualities,
he who had braved countless battles, weathered
the thunder when warrior troops clashed together,
saw a stone arch set in the cliff
through which a stream spurted; steam rose
from the boiling water; he could not stay long
in the hollow near the hoard for fear
of being scorched by the dragon's flames.

Then, such was his fury, the leader of the Geats
threw out his chest and gave a great roar,
the brave man bellowed; his voice, renowned
in battle, hammered the grey rock's anvil.
The guardian of the hoard knew the voice for human;
violent hatred stirred within him. Now no time
remained to entreat for peace. At once
the monster's breath, burning battle vapour,
issued from the barrow; the earth itself snarled.
The lord of the Geats, standing under the cliff,
raised his shield against the fearsome stranger;
then that sinuous creature spoiled
for the fight. The brave and warlike king
had already drawn his keen-edged sword,
(it was an ancient heirloom); a terror of each other
lurked in the hearts of the two antagonists.
While the winged creature coiled himself up,
the friend and lord of men stood unflinching
by his shield; Beowulf waited ready armed.
    Then, fiery and twisted, the dragon swiftly
shrithed towards its fate. The shield protected
the life and body of the famous prince
for far less time than he had looked for.

It was the first occasion in all his life
that fate did not decree triumph for him
in battle. The lord of the Geats raised
his arm, and struck the mottled monster
with his vast ancestral sword; but the bright blade's
edge was blunted by the bone, bit
less keenly than the desperate king required.
The defender of the barrow bristled with anger
at the blow, spouted murderous fire, so that flames
leaped through the air. The gold-friend of the Geats
did not boast of famous victories; his proven sword,
the blade bared in battle, had failed him
as it ought not to have done. That great Ecgtheow's
greater son had to journey on from this world
was no pleasant matter; much against his will,
he was obliged to make his dwelling
elsewhere — sooner or later every man must leave
this transitory life. It was not long
before the fearsome ones closed again.
The guardian of the hoard was filled with fresh hope,
his breast was heaving; he who had ruled a nation
suffered agony, surrounded by flame.
And Beowulf's companions, sons of nobles —

so far from protecting him in a troop together,
unflinching in the fight — shrank back into the forest
scared for their own lives. One man alone
obeyed his conscience. The claims of kinship
can never be ignored by a right-minded man.

   His name was Wiglaf, a noble warrior,
Weohstan's son, kinsman of Ælfhere,
a leader of the Swedes; he saw that his lord,
helmeted, was tormented by the intense heat.
Then he recalled the honours Beowulf had bestowed
on him — the wealthy citadel of the Wægmundings,
the rights to land his father owned before him.
He could not hold back then; he grasped the round,
yellow shield; he drew his ancient sword,
reputed to be the legacy of Eanmund,
Ohthere's son.

              Weohstan had slain him
in a skirmish while Eanmund was a wanderer,
a friendless man, and then had carried off
to his own kinsmen the gleaming helmet,
the linked corslet, the ancient sword
forged by giants. It was Onela,
Eanmund's uncle, who gave him that armour,

ready for use; but Onela did not refer to the feud,
though Weohstan had slain his brother's son.
For many years Weohstan owned that war-gear,
sword and corslet, until his son was old enough
to achieve great feats as he himself had done.
Then, when Weohstan journeyed on from the earth,
an old man, he left Wiglaf – who was
with the Geats – a great legacy of armour
of every kind.

                This was the first time
the young warrior had weathered the battle storm,
standing at the shoulder of his lord.
His courage did not melt, nor did his kinsman's sword
fail him in the fight. The dragon found that out
when they met in mortal combat.
    Wiglaf spoke, constantly reminding
his companions of their duty – he was mournful.
'I think of that evening we emptied the mead-cup
in the feasting-hall, partook and pledged our lord,
who presented us with rings, that we would repay him
for his gifts of armour, helmets and hard swords,
if ever the need, need such as this, arose.
For this very reason he asked us

to join with him in this journey, deemed us
worthy of renown, and gave me these treasures;
he looked on us as loyal warriors,
brave in battle; even so, our lord,
guardian of the Geats, intended to perform
this feat alone, because of all men
he had achieved the greatest exploits,
daring deeds. Now the day has come
when our lord needs support, the might
of strong men; let us hurry forward
and help our leader as long as fire remains,
fearsome, searing flames. God knows
I would rather that fire embraced my body
beside the charred body of my gold-giver;
it seems wrong to me that we should shoulder
our shields, carry them home afterwards,
unless we can first kill the venomous foe,
guard the prince of the Geats, I know
in my heart his feats of old were such
that he should not now be the only Geat to suffer
and fall in combat; in common we shall share
sword, helmet, corslet, the trappings of war.'
    Then that man fought his way through the fumes,

went helmeted to help his lord. He shouted out:
'Brave Beowulf, may success attend you —
for in the days when you were young, you swore
that so long as you lived you would never allow
your fame to decay; now, O resolute king,
renowned for your exploits, you must guard your life
with all your skill. I shall assist you.'
    At this the seething dragon attacked a second time;
shimmering with fire the venomous visitor fell on his foes,
the men he loathed. With waves of flame, he burnt
the shield right up to its boss; Wiglaf's
corslet afforded him no protection whatsoever.
But the young warrior still fought bravely, sheltered
behind his kinsman's shield after his own
was consumed by flames. Still the battle-king
set his mind on deeds of glory; with prodigious strength
he struck a blow so violent that his sword stuck
in the dragon's skull. But Nægling snapped!
Beowulf's old grey-hued sword
failed him in the fight. Fate did not ordain
that the iron edge should assist him
in that struggle; Beowulf's hand was too strong.
Indeed I have been told that he overtaxed

each and every weapon, hardened by blood, that he bore
into battle; his own great strength betrayed him.
    Then the dangerous dragon, scourge of the Geats,
was intent a third time upon attack; he rushed
at the renowned man when he saw an opening;
fiery, battle-grim, he gripped the hero's neck
between his sharp teeth; Beowulf was bathed
in blood; it spurted out in streams.
Then, I have heard, the loyal thane
alongside the Geatish king displayed great courage,
strength and daring, as was his nature.
To assist his kinsman, that man in mail
aimed not for the head but lunged at the belly
of their vile enemy (in so doing his hand
was badly burnt); his sword, gleaming and adorned,
sank in up to the hilt and at once the flames
began to abate. The king still had control then
over his senses; he drew the deadly knife,
keen-edged in battle, that he wore on his corslet;
then the lord of the Geats dispatched the dragon.
Thus they had killed their enemy — their courage
enabled them — the brave kinsmen together
had destroyed him. Such should a man,

a thane, be in time of necessity!

                           That was the last
of all the king's achievements, his last
exploit in the world. Then the wound
the earth-dragon had inflicted with his teeth
began to burn and swell; very soon he
was suffering intolerable pain as the poison
boiled within him. Then the wise leader
tottered forward and slumped on a seat
by the barrow; he gazed at the work of giants,
saw how the ancient earthwork contained
stone arches supported by columns.
Then, with his own hands, the best of thanes
refreshed the renowned prince with water,
washed his friend and lord, blood-stained
and battle-weary, and unfastened his helmet.

    Beowulf began to speak, he defied
his mortal injury; he was well aware
that his life's course, with all its delights,
had come to an end; his days on earth
were exhausted, death drew very close:
'It would have made me happy, at this time,
to pass on war-gear to my son, had I

been granted an heir to succeed me,
sprung of my seed. I have ruled the Geats
for fifty winters; no king of any
neighbouring tribe has dared to attack me
with swords, or sought to cow and subdue me.
But in my own home I have awaited
my destiny, cared well for my dependants,
and I have not sought trouble, or sworn
any oaths unjustly. Because of all these things
I can rejoice, drained now by death-wounds;
for the Ruler of Men will have no cause to blame me
after I have died on the count that I deprived
other kinsmen of their lives. Now hurry,
dear Wiglaf; rummage the hoard
under the grey rock, for the dragon sleeps,
riddled with wounds, robbed of his treasure.
Be as quick as you can so that I may see
the age-old store of gold, and examine
all the priceless, shimmering stones; once I
have set eyes on such a store, it will be
more easy for me to die, to abandon
the life and land that have so long been mine.'

    Then, I have been told, as soon as he heard

the words of his lord, wounded in battle,
Wiglaf hastened into the earth-cavern,
still wearing his corslet, his woven coat of mail.
After the fierce warrior, flushed with victory,
had walked past a daïs, he came upon
the hoard — a hillock of precious stones,
and gold treasure glowing on the ground;
he saw wondrous wall-hangings; the lair
of the serpent, the aged twilight-flier;
and the stoups and vessels of a people
long dead, now lacking a polisher,
deprived of adornments. There were many old,
rusty helmets, and many an armlet
cunningly wrought. A treasure hoard,
gold in the ground, will survive its owner
easily, whosoever hides it!
And he saw also hanging high
over the hoard a standard fashioned with gold strands,
a miracle of handiwork; a light shone from it,
by which he was able to distinguish the earth
and look at the adornments. There was no sign
of the serpent, the sword had savaged and slain him.
Then I heard that Wiglaf rifled the hoard

in the barrow, the antique work of giants —
he chose and carried off as many cups and salvers
as he could, and he also took the standard,
the incomparable banner; Beowulf's sword,
iron-edged, had injured
the guardian of the hoard, he who had held it
through the ages and fought to defend it
with flames — terrifying, blistering,
ravening at midnight — until he was slain.
Wiglaf hurried on his errand, eager to return,
spurred on by the treasures; in his heart he was troubled
whether he would find the prince of the Geats,
so grievously wounded, still alive
in the place where he had left him.
Then at last he came, carrying the treasures,
to the renowned king; his lord's life-blood
was ebbing; once more he splashed him
with water, until Beowulf revived a little,
began to frame his thoughts.
                              Gazing at the gold,
the warrior, the sorrowing king, said:
'With these words I thank
the King of Glory, the Eternal Lord,

the Ruler, for all the treasures here before me,
that in my lifetime I have been able
to gain them for the Geats.
And now that I have bartered my old life
for this treasure hoard, you must serve
and inspire our people. I will not long be with you.
Command the battle-warriors, after the funeral fire,
to build a fine barrow overlooking the sea;
let it tower high on Whaleness
as a reminder to my people.
And let it be known as *Beowulf's barrow*
to all seafarers, to men who steer their ships
from far over the swell and the saltspray.'
    Then the prince, bold of mind, detached
his golden collar and gave it to Wiglaf,
the young spear-warrior, and also his helmet
adorned with gold, his ring and his corslet,
and enjoined him to use them well;
'You are the last survivor of our family,
the Wægmundings; fate has swept
all my kinsmen, those courageous warriors,
to their doom. I must follow them.'
    Those were the warrior's last words

before he succumbed to the raging flames
on the pyre; his soul migrated from his breast
to meet the judgement of righteous men.

Then it was harrowing for the young hero
that he should have to see that beloved man
lying on the earth at his life's end,
wracked by pain. His slayer lay
there too, himself slain, the terrible
cave-dragon. That serpent, coiled evilly,
could no longer guard the gold-hoard,
but blades of iron, beaten and tempered
by smiths, notched in battle, had taken him off;
his wings were clipped now, he lay
mortally wounded, motionless on the earth
at the mound's entrance. No more did he fly
through the night sky, or spread his wings,
proud of his possessions; but he lay prostrate
because of the power of Beowulf, their leader.
Truly, I have heard that no hero of the Geats,
no fire-eater, however daring, could quell
the scorching blast of that venomous one
and lay his hands on the hoard in the lair,
should he find its sentinel waiting there,

watching over the barrow. Beowulf paid
the price of death for that mighty hoard;
both he and the dragon had travelled to the end
of this transitory life.

Not long after that
the lily-livered ones slunk out of the wood;
ten cowardly oath-breakers, who had lacked
the courage to let fly with their spears
as their lord so needed, came forward together;
overcome with shame, they carried their shields
and weapons to where their leader lay;
they gazed at Wiglaf. That warrior, bone-weary,
knelt beside the shoulders of his lord; he tried
to rouse him with water; it was all in vain.
For all his efforts, his longing, he could not
detain the life of his leader on earth,
or alter anything the Ruler ordained.
God in His wisdom governed the deeds
of all men, as He does now.

Then the young warrior was not at a loss
for well-earned, angry words for those cowards.
Wiglaf, Weohstan's son, sick at heart,
eyed those faithless men and said:

'He who does not wish to disguise the truth
can indeed say that — when it was a question
not of words but war — our lord completely wasted
the treasures he gave you, the same war-gear
you stand in over there, helmets and corslets
the prince presented often to his thanes on the ale-bench
in the feasting-hall, the very finest weapons
he could secure from far and wide.
The king of the Geats had no need to bother
with boasts about his battle-companions;
yet God, Giver of Victories, granted
that he should avenge himself with his sword
single-handed, when all his courage was called for.
I could hardly begin to guard his life
in the fight; but all the same I attempted
to help my kinsman beyond my power.
Each time I slashed at that deadly enemy,
he was a little weaker, the flames leaped
less fiercely from his jaws. Too few defenders
rallied round our prince when he was most pressed.
Now you and your dependants can no longer delight
in gifts of swords, or take pleasure in property,
a happy home; but, after thanes from far and wide

have heard of your flight, your shameful cowardice,
each of your male kinsmen will be condemned
to become a wanderer, an exile deprived
of the land he owns. For every warrior
death is better than dark days of disgrace.'
    Then Wiglaf ordered that Beowulf's great feat
be proclaimed in the stronghold, up along the cliff-edge,
where a troop of shield-warriors had waited all morning,
wondering sadly if their dear lord was dead,
or if he would return.
                    The man who galloped
to the headland gave them the news at once;
he kept back nothing but called out:
'The lord of the Geats, he who gave joy
to all our people, lies rigid on his death-bed;
slaughtered by the dragon, he now sleeps;
and his deadly enemy, slashed by the knife,
sleeps beside him: he was quite unable
to wound the serpent with a sword. Wiglaf,
son of Weohstan, sits by Beowulf,
the quick and the dead — both brave men —
side by side; weary in his heart
he watches over friend and foe alike.

Now the Geats must make ready for a time
of war, for the Franks and the Frisians,
in far-off regions, will hear soon
of the king's death. Our feud with the Franks
grew worse when Hygelac sailed with his fleet
to the shores of Frisia. Frankish warriors
attacked him there, and outfought him,
bravely forced the king in his corslet
to give ground; he fell, surrounded
by his retainers; that prince presented
not one ornament to his followers. Since then,
the king of the Franks has been no friend of ours.
　　Nor would I in the least rely on peace
or honesty from the Swedish people; everyone
remembers how Ongentheow slew Hæthcyn,
Hrethel's son, in battle near Ravenswood
when, rashly, the Geats first attacked the Swedes.
At once Ongentheow, Ohthere's father,
old but formidable, retaliated; he killed
Hæthcyn, and released his wife from captivity,
set free the mother of Onela and Ohthere,
an aged woman bereft of all her ornaments;
and then he pursued his mortal enemies

until, lordless, with utmost difficulty,
they reached and found refuge in Ravenswood.
Then Ongentheow, with a huge army, penned in
those warriors, exhausted by wounds,
who had escaped the sword; all night long
he shouted fearsome threats at those shivering thanes,
swore that in the morning he and his men would let
their blood in streams with sharp-edged swords,
and string some up on gallows-trees
as sport for birds. Just as day dawned
those despairing men were afforded relief;
they heard the joyful song of Hygelac's
horn and trumpet as that hero came,
hurrying to their rescue with a band of retainers.
After that savage, running battle, the soil
was blood-stained, scuffled, a sign of how
the Swedes and the Geats fomented their feud.
Then Ongentheow, old and heavy-hearted,
headed for his stronghold with his retainers,
that resolute man retreated; he realized
how spirit and skill combined in the person
of proud Hygelac; he had no confidence
about the outcome of an open fight with the seafarers,

the Geatish warriors, in defence of his hoard,
his wife and children; the old man thus withdrew
behind an earth-wall. Then the Swedes were pursued,
Hygelac's banner was hoisted over that earth-work
after the Geats, sons of Hrethel, had stormed
the stronghold. Then grey-haired Ongentheow
was cornered by swords, the king of the Swedes
was constrained to face and suffer his fate
as Eofor willed it. Wulf, the son
of Wonred, slashed angrily at Ongentheow
with his sword, so that blood spurted
from the veins under his hair. The old Swede,
king of his people, was not afraid
but as soon as he had regained his balance
repaid that murderous blow with interest.
Then Wonred's daring son could no longer
lift his hand against the aged warrior
but, with that stroke, Ongentheow had sheared
right through his helmet so that Wulf, blood-stained,
was thrown to the ground; he was not yet doomed to die
but later recovered from that grievous wound.
When Wulf collapsed, his brother Eofor,
Hygelac's brave thane, swung his broad sword,

made by giants, shattered the massive helmet
above the raised shield; Ongentheow fell,
the guardian of the people was fatally wounded.
Then many warriors quickly rescued Wulf,
and bandaged his wounds, once they had won control
(as fate decreed) of that field of corpses.
Meanwhile Eofor stripped Ongentheow's body
of its iron corslet, wrenched the helmet from his head,
the mighty sword from his hands;
he carried the old man's armour to Hygelac.
He received those battle adornments, honourably
promised to reward Eofor above other men;
he kept his word; the king of the Geats,
Hrethel's son, repaid Eofor and Wulf
for all they had accomplished with outstanding gifts
when he had returned home; he gave each of them
land and interlocked rings to the value
of a hundred thousand pence — no man on earth
had cause to blame the brothers for accepting
such wealth, they had earned it by sheer audacity.
Then, as a pledge of friendship, Hygelac gave
Eofor his only daughter to grace his home.

    That is the history of hatred and feud

and deadly enmity; and because of it,
I expect the Swedes to attack us
as soon as they hear our lord is lifeless —
he who in earlier days defended a land
and its treasure against two monstrous enemies
after the death of its heroes, daring Scyldings,
he who protected the people, and achieved feats
all but impossible.

                Let us lose no time now
but go and gaze there upon our king
and carry him, who gave us rings,
to the funeral pyre. And let us not grudge gold
to melt with that bold man, for we have a mighty hoard,
a mint of precious metal, bought with pain;
and now, from this last exploit, a harvest
he paid for with his own life; these the fire
shall devour, the ravening flames embrace.
No thane shall wear or carry these treasures
in his memory, no fair maiden shall hang
an ornament of interlinked rings at her throat,
but often and again, desolate, deprived of gold,
they must tread the paths of exile,
now that their lord has laid aside laughter,

festivity, happiness. Henceforth, fingers must grasp,
hands must hold, many a spear
chill with the cold of morning; no sound of the harp
shall rouse the warriors but, craving for carrion,
the dark raven shall have its say, and tell
the eagle how it fared at the feast when it vied
with the wolf to lay bare the bones of corpses.'

Thus the brave messenger told of and foretold
harrowing times; and he was not far wrong.
Those events were fated. Every man in the troop
stood up, stained with tears, and set out
for Eagleness to see that strange spectacle.
There they found him lifeless on the sand,
the soft bed where he slept, who often before
had given them rings; that good man's days
on earth were ended; the warrior-king,
lord of the Geats, had died a wondrous death.
But first they saw a strange creature
there, a loathsome serpent lying
nearby; the fire-dragon, fierce
and mottled, was scorched by its own flames.
It measured fifty paces from head to tail;
sometimes it had soared at night

through the cool air, then dived
to its dark lair; now it lay rigid in death,
no longer to haunt caverns under the earth.
Goblets and vessels stood by it,
salvers and valuable swords, eaten through
by rust, as if they had lain
for a thousand winters in the earth's embrace.
That mighty legacy, gold of men long dead,
lay under a curse; it was enchanted
so that no human might enter
the cavern save him to whom God,
the true Giver of Victories, Guardian of Men,
granted permission to plunder the hoard –
whichever warrior seemed worthy to Him.

Then it was clear that, whoever devised it,
the evil scheme of hiding the hoard under the rock
had come to nothing; the guardian had killed
a brave and famous man; that feud
was violently avenged. The day that a warrior,
renowned for his courage, will reach the end (as fate
    ordains) of his life on earth,
that hour when a man may feast in the hall
with his friends no longer, is always unpredictable.

It was thus with Beowulf when he tracked down
and attacked the barrow's guardian; he himself
was not aware how he would leave this world.
The glorious princes who first placed that gold there
had solemnly pronounced that until domesday
any man attempting to plunder the hoard
should be guilty of wickedness, confined,
tormented and tortured by the devil himself.
Never before had Beowulf been granted
such a wealth of gold by the gracious Lord.

Wiglaf, the son of Weohstan, said:
'Many thanes must often suffer
because of the will of one, as we do now.
We could not dissuade the king we loved,
or in any way restrain the lord of our land
from not drawing his sword against the gold-warden,
from not letting him lie where he had long lain
and remain in his lair until the world's end;
but he fulfilled his high destiny. The hoard,
so grimly gained, is now easy of access;
our king was driven there by too harsh a fate.
I took the path under the earth-wall,
entered the hall and examined all

the treasures after the dragon deserted it;
I was hardly invited there. Hurriedly
I grasped as many treasures as I could,
a huge burden, and carried them here
to my king; he was still alive then,
conscious and aware of this world around him.
He found words for his thronging thoughts,
born of sorrow, asked me to salute you,
said that as a monument to your lord's exploits
you should build a great and glorious barrow
over his pyre, for he of all men
was the most famous warrior on the wide earth
for as long as he lived, happy in his stronghold.
Now let us hurry once more together
and see the hoard of priceless stones,
that wonder under the wall; I will lead you
so that you will come sufficiently close
to the rings, the solid gold. After we
get back, let us quickly build the bier,
and then let us carry our king,
the man we loved, to where he must
long remain in the Lord's protection.'
    Then the brave warrior, Weohstan's son,

directed that orders be given to many men
(to all who owned houses, elders of the people)
to fetch wood from far to place beneath
their prince on the funeral pyre:

'Now flames,
the blazing fire, must devour the lord of warriors
who often endured the iron-tipped arrow-shower,
when the dark cloud loosed by bow strings
broke above the shield-wall, quivering;
when the eager shaft, with its feather garb,
discharged its duty to the barb.'

I have heard that Weohstan's wise son
summoned from Beowulf's band his seven
best thanes, and went with those warriors
into the evil grotto; the man leading
the way grasped a brand. Then those retainers
were not hesitant about rifling the hoard
as soon as they set eyes on any part of it,
lying unguarded, gradually rusting,
in that rock cavern; no man was conscience-stricken
about carrying out those priceless treasures
as quickly as he could. Also, they pushed the dragon,
the serpent over the precipice; they let the waves take him,

the dark waters embrace the warden of the hoard.
Then the wagon was laden with twisted gold,
with treasures of every kind, and the king,
the old battle-warrior, was borne to Whaleness.
Then, on the headland, the Geats prepared

a mighty pyre
for Beowulf, hung round with helmets and shields
and shining mail, in accordance with his wishes;
and then the mourning warriors laid
their dear lord, the famous prince, upon it.

And there on Whaleness, the heroes kindled
the most mighty of pyres; the dark wood-smoke
soared over the fire, the roaring flames
mingled with weeping — the winds' tumult subsided —
until the body became ash, consumed even
to its core. The heart's cup overflowed;
they mourned their loss, the death of their lord.
And, likewise, a maiden of the Geats,
with her tresses swept up, intoned
a dirge for Beowulf time after time,
declared she lived in dread of days to come
dark with carnage and keening, terror of the enemy,
humiliation and captivity.

Heaven swallowed the smoke.
Then the Geats built a barrow on the headland —
it was high and broad, visible from far
to all seafarers; in ten days they built the beacon
for that courageous man; and they constructed
as noble an enclosure as wise men
could devise, to enshrine the ashes.
They buried rings and brooches in the barrow,
all those adornments that brave men
had brought out from the hoard after Beowulf died.
They bequeathed the gleaming gold,
                                treasure of men,
to the earth, and there it still remains
as useless as it was before.

Then twelve brave warriors, sons of heroes,
rode round the barrow, sorrowing;
they mourned their king, chanted
an elegy, spoke about that great man:
they exalted his heroic life, lauded
his daring deeds; it is fitting for a man,
when his lord and friend must leave this life,
to mouth words in his praise
and to cherish his memory.
Thus the Geats, his hearth-companions,
grieved over the death of their lord;
they said that of all kings on earth
he was the kindest, the most gentle,
the most just to his people, the most eager for fame.

ELUCIDATORY NOTES

Page 46 *Scyld Scefing . . . had been found a waif.* Scyld, the eponymous hero of the Scyldings or Danes, arrived mysteriously in Denmark: a boy in a boat. The poem begins with his funeral and ends with the funeral of Beowulf, both men saviours of the Danes.

Page 47 *Beow of Denmark . . .* This passage both establishes the identity of the Danish royal house and glorifies it. One effect of this is to make Beowulf's exploits look all the more lustrous.

Page 48 *Heorot* Literally 'hart' or 'stag', a beast symbolic of kingship. The Danish royal seat was at Leire on the island of Zealand.

fierce tongues of loathsome fire . . . Heorot was probably burned down in a feud between the Danes and Heathobards. The 'father- and son-in-law' are Hrothgar and Ingeld. This passage, following immediately after the glorification of Heorot, is a good example of the poet's skill at dramatic contrast, as well as exemplifying the way in which he often anticipates later developments.

one of the seed of Cain The Anglo-Saxons believed that the giants mentioned in *Genesis* 6:4 were descended from Cain. The poet gives Grendel a quasi-historical pedigree, and stature, by relating him to them.

Page 50 *wergild* Literally, 'man-money'. Compensation paid to a victim's family.

shrithe I have derived this word from *scrian: to glide, to sidle (rhyme with 'writhe')*.

Page 54 *the boar crest . . .* A helmet found at Benty Grange in Derbyshire is topped with a boar-figure. The boar was sacred to the god Freyr and to wear it perhaps implies a warrior fought with his protection.

Page 56 *a prince of the Vandals* That Wulfgar was serving at the Danish Court seems to exemplify Beowulf's later comment, made in another context, that 'Strong men should seek fame in far-off lands'.

Page 59 *Beowulf, my friend . . .* Beowulf has presented himself to Hrothgar as a man with supernatural strength, sent by his people to Denmark because he alone is capable of delivering the Danes from their torment. But Hrothgar (as discussed in 'The Social Background') acknowledges his arrival as a matter of obligation because Hrothgar had taken in Beowulf's father, Ecgtheow, and given treasures on his behalf to settle a feud.

Page 60 *Ecglaf's son Unferth . . . unlocked his thoughts* Unferth literally means 'un-peace', i.e. conflict. The character who taunts the hero, and is his foil, is common to many heroic poems.

Page 66 *we, this night, shall forgo the use of weapons . . .* Beowulf's renunciation of weapons is magnanimous and makes his victory (when it comes) all the greater. But an unarmed fight between hero and monster is also central to the folk-tale that was one of the poet's sources.

Page 67 *he hungrily seized a sleeping warrior . . .* Later in the poem, the poet tells us this warrior was called Hondscio (literally 'hand-shoe', i.e. glove).

Page 68 *unless it were gutted by greedy tongues of flames . . .* It was! So this is a deft piece of dramatic irony.

Page 70 *When Beowulf, brave in battle, placed hand, arm and shoulder . . .* The poet later tells us that Grendel's talon was nailed up on the inside of a gable.

Page 71 *He recounted all he knew of Sigemund . . .* Why does Hrothgar's thane choose to sing about Sigemund and Heremod? The poem's original audience would doubtless have been quite clear about the meaning of these allusions. In appearing to compare Beowulf to Sigemund, a great compliment must be intended (for Sigemund was one of the greatest Northern heroes), but in describing a dragon-fight the poet is also ironically foreshadowing the way in which Beowulf himself will die. Heremod is held up as a warning, perhaps – a man who misuses his personal strength and fails his people.

Page 75 *the time was not yet come* . . . The poet is foreshadowing the time when Hrothgar's nephew Hrothulf was treacherous to the king, and later deposed Hrothgar's son Hrethric.

Page 76 *He sang of Finn's troop* . . . This long allusive passage describes how the Half-Dane Hnaef and his sister's son were killed at Finnesburh because of the treachery of the Jutes. The new leader of the Half-Danes, Hengest, swears to serve Finn, and Finn undertakes to be generous to the Half-Danes. But Hengest is brooding on vengeance and, after Guthlaf and Oslaf arrive from Denmark, the fire is fanned into flames. Now Finn is killed and the Danes go home with treasures, also taking with them Hildeburh, who has lost her husband, her son and her brother. The poet may intend a comparison between Hildeburh and Wealhtheow (who will later be a victim of Hrothulf's treachery), and to show that tribal enmity is greater than any peace-weaving marriage; he may also be suggesting in a more general way that the Danes' joy today will give way to grief tomorrow.

Page 80 *Hrothgar and Hrothulf were sitting side by side* . . . Another foreshadowing of Hrothulf's later treachery. The irony is compounded by Wealhtheow's misplaced confidence twenty lines later.

Page 81 *be kind in your counsel to these boys* Wealhtheow's two sons, Hrethric and Hrothmund.

Page 88 *Hrunting, the long-hilted sword . . . twig-like patterning* Fine swords were not only very highly valued possessions but were sometimes given names. The beautiful 'twig-like' decoration simply derives from the pattern-welding of soft pure iron and steely iron to make a reliable blade.

Page 92 *Then the ninth hour came* . . . Not too much should be read into this solitary and startling echo of the Crucifixion. While it is true that Beowulf has purged the lake it is unlikely that the poet was trying to portray him as a Christ-figure.

Page 95 *when the tide of rising water* . . . The biblical Flood that drowned all the descendants of Cain.

it was recorded in runic letters . . . The alphabet sometimes known from its first letters as the *Futhark*, made up of vertical and diagonal strokes. Runes had a magical significance but were also used for the purposes of commemoration and identification.

Page 96 *Heremod was hardly that to Ecgwala's sons* . . . This is the second reference to Heremod (the first was in the Sigemund digression, see p. 72) and again he is held up as a warning.

Page 102 *Queen Thryth was proud* . . . The purpose of this digression is obscure. Maybe the real comparison is not between Hygd and Thryth but between Hygelac and Offa. Proceeding from the assumption of wordplay (Hygd: thought – Hygelac: lack of thought), Howell Chickering argues that 'the point of the contrast is this . . . while a strong and wise king can bring a vicious queen under control, a wise queen can do little about her lord's lack of wisdom or his misuse of strength'.

Page 105 *she is promised to Froda's noble son* . . . Here the poet returns to one of his *leitmotifs*: the inefficacy of peace-weaving marriages when confronted by virulent tribal enmity.

Page 110 *and when the warlike Swedes, savage warriors* . . . This is the first fleeting reference to the long-running conflict between the Geats and the Swedes. This conflict is the subject of the main digressions in the remainder of the poem.

Page 115 *That grim combat in which Hygelac was slain* . . . Hygelac was killed while leading a raid on the Frisian territory of the Franks in about AD 525.

Page 116 *Two exiles, Ohthere's sons* . . . When Onela became king of the Swedes, two of his nephews, Eanmund and Eadgils, sought refuge at the Geatish court of Heardred. As a result, Onela attacked Heardred, and killed him. Eanmund was also killed (by Weohstan), but Eadgils survived and, with Beowulf's help, avenged his brother's death by killing Onela. It follows that Eadgils succeeded Onela as king of the Swedes.

Page 122 *His name was Wiglaf* Wiglaf was by blood half-Swede and half-Geat. He and Beowulf were both members of the Waegmunding family.

Weohstan had slain him . . . The circumstances of Eanmund's death are described in the note above (*Two exiles, Ohthere's sons* . . .). The fact that Weohstan slew Eanmund and that Eanmund's brother had succeeded to the Swedish throne, may explain why Weohstan and his son Wiglaf settled in Geatland. They would have been *persona non grata* amongst the Swedes.

Page 124 *he burnt the shield* . . . Probably made of linden wood.

But Naegling snapped!   Beowulf's sword, like Unferth's sword Hrunting, had its own name.

Page 126   *he gazed at the work of giants . . .*   In Old English poetry, 'giants' is sometimes a synonym for 'Romans', because they knew how to build in stone. Here, the poet has in mind 'stone-builders' and is thinking of the 'noble people' who concealed the treasure in the cave.

Page 128   *the antique work of giants . . .*   And here, 'giants' can only mean the 'noble people' who had made the treasure.

Page 132   *Now the Geats must make ready . . .*   Beowulf is dead and in the long passage that now follows, the messenger anticipates that the Franks and Swedes will close in on their old enemy, the Geats. The poet explains why by referring to Hygelac's earlier attack on the Franks in Frisia and to 'the history of hatred and feud and deadly enmity' between Geats and Swedes that culminated in the death of the Swedish king, Ongentheow.

Page 135   *craving for carrion, the dark raven . . .*   The raven, the eagle and the wolf are the traditional beasts of battle in Old English poetry. They are brought into play here with uncommon skill.

Page 136   *That mighty legacy, gold of men long dead, lay under a curse . . . by the gracious Lord.*   This is clearly an important passage, much fought over by critics. It appears that Beowulf has unwittingly fallen a victim to the curse on the gold; and yet, paradoxically, God has been on his side and given him 'permission to plunder the hoard'. Maybe the fact that Beowulf does not appear to know the gold is cursed exonerates him. The last word of the passage can also be translated 'owner'.

Many thanes must often suffer because of the will of one . . .   The 'one' in question may be Beowulf and may be the slave who stole the precious cup. If it is Beowulf, then one has to decide whether the poet is criticizing Beowulf as an individual; or saying that by definition heroes are larger than life, and thoroughly uncomfortable to live with; or suggesting a deficiency in the heroic code within which Beowulf operates.

Page 138   *a maiden of the Geats . . .*   The motion of the poem is cyclical. It began in darkness and now that Beowulf is dead, and the Franks and Swedes are poised to attack, the darkness is shown to be closing in once more.

PICTURE ACKNOWLEDGEMENTS

Antikvarisk-Topografiska Arkivet 19;
Bristol Cathedral 34L;
By kind permission of the Trustees of the British Museum 23, 34R;
British Museum/Photoresources 12, 22, 26, 27;
Dean and Chapter Library, Durham/Phaidon Press Ltd Archives 33;
Department of Environment 54/5, 56/7, 80/1, 102/3, 104/5, 106/7, 108/9, 118/19;
Marianne Majerus 2/3, 4/5, 6/7, 10/11, 16/17, 20, 24/5, 30/1, 32, 46/7, 52/3, 58/9, 60/1, 62/3, 64/5, 66/7, 94/5, 96/7, 98/9, 100/1, 104/5, 106/7, 108/9, 138/9;
Museum of National Antiquities, Stockholm/Photoresources 17;
National Museum Copenhagen/Photoresources 14, 21, 45;
Photoresources 11;
Sonia Halliday and Laura Lushington 18, 72/3, 74/5, 76/7;
University Historical Museum, Oslo/Photoresources 8, 13R;
Yorkshire Museum 13L.

INDEX   Page numbers in *italics* refer to illustrations